How to Solve
Conflicts

How to Solve Conflicts

by
George Sweeting

❧ ❧ ❧

MOODY PRESS
CHICAGO

Moody Paperback Edition, 1975

Seventh Printing, 1977

ISBN: 0-8024-3654-4

The use of selected references from various versions of
the Bible in this publication does not necessarily imply
publisher endorsement of the versions in their entirety.

Moody Press, a ministry of the Moody Bible Institute, is
designed for education, evangelization and edification.
If we may assist you in knowing more about Christ and
the Christian life, please write us without obligation to:
Moody Press, c/o MLM, Chicago, Illinois 60610.

Printed in the United States of America

To

all the exciting students
of the Moody Bible Institute,
past and present,
who are concerned and involved
in reaching our world

WITH APPRECIATION TO

Mark Sweeney,
Executive Producer of "Moody Presents,"
the international radio voice
of Moody Bible Institute,
for his assistance in editing
these studies for book form

Contents

Preface

The epistle of James stands out as one of the most practical books in the entire New Testament. This brief letter, written by the brother of our Lord, presents the Christian life as it ought to be lived by every believer.

Written to the Christians of the first century, the book of James is a letter of encouragement as well as instruction to those who stood in the very midst of conflict. It speaks to the many and varied needs of people who had been scattered throughout the Roman Empire by persecution.

The theme of this epistle is practical faith—faith that is dynamic and alive, faith in action. Because he is writing to Christians, James is concerned about conduct, not creed; about behavior, not belief. His purpose is to take the Christian beyond the stage of "easy believism" and to introduce him to a vital and genuine faith that demonstrates itself in a tangible way.

James speaks to Christians where they are: in the midst of trial and conflict, experiencing testing and temptation, and inhabiting a strife-torn world. He gives practical solutions to everyday problems that all believers experience. He deals with the nitty-gritty of life, and he tells us that a faith that *works* is a faith that *lasts*.

The epistle of James is extremely practical. Its five chapters are packed with simple yet profound truths which can aid you in your Christian life. It is not an easy book, because it minces no words. But it will serve as a source of great blessing to you as you diligently seek to become a doer of the Word.

This book is written with the expressed purpose of stimulating you to further study of the epistle of James. It is not intended to be a full commentary on the epistle, but rather a practical discussion of the principle topics James deals with in his letter. I trust that the following chapters will be helpful to you as you "put feet to your faith" in your daily walk with Christ.

How to Solve Conflicts

My brethren, count it all joy when ye fall into divers temptations;

Knowing this, that the trying of your faith worketh patience.

But let patience have her perfect work, that ye may be perfect and entire, wanting nothing.

If any of you lack wisdom, let him ask of God, that giveth to all men liberally, and upbraideth not; and it shall be given him.

But let him ask in faith, nothing wavering. For he that wavereth is like a wave of the sea driven with the wind and tossed.

For let not that man think that he shall receive any thing of the Lord.

A double minded man is unstable in all his ways.

Let the brother of low degree rejoice in that he is exalted:

But the rich, in that he is made low: because as the flower of the grass he shall pass away.

For the sun is no sooner risen with a burning heat, but it withereth the grass, and the flower thereof falleth, and the grace of the fashion of it perisheth: so also shall the rich man fade away in his ways.

Blessed is the man that endureth temptation: for when he is tried, he shall receive the crown of life, which the Lord hath promised to them that love him.

JAMES 1:2-12

1

Turning Trials into Triumph

JAMES 1:2-12

Times of trial can be turned into triumph!

Webster's dictionary defines happiness as "a state of well-being" and "a pleasurable satisfaction." Many people in our world today feel that happiness is a state of mind which they seldom experience. Pressures at home and on the job, personal problems—all blend together to rob the average person of true and lasting happiness.

The Bible tells us that for the child of God happiness can be a living reality. And more than that—the Christian can be triumphant during times of great trials.

There are three things to remember concerning trials:

1. Trials are the common experience of all of us. No one is immune. Trials are a part of living.
2. Trials are transitory. C. B. Williams translates 1 Peter 1:6 this way: "In such a hope keep on rejoicing, although for a little while you must be sorrow-stricken with various trials." Trials, though difficult, are "for a little while."
3. Trials are lessons that shouldn't be wasted. Though not enjoyable or necessarily good in themselves, trials constitute a divine work for our ultimate good. Jesus never promised an easy journey, but He did promise a safe landing. The poet asks,

13

> When each earthly prop gives under,
> And life seems a restless sea,
> Are you then a God-kept wonder,
> Satisfied and calm and free?
>
> *Streams in the Desert*

Shortly before the ascension into heaven, Jesus gave His disciples some great words of encouragement. "In the world," said Jesus, "ye shall have tribulation: but be of good cheer; I have overcome the world" (Jn 16:33). Tribulation is followed by triumph. Crowns are formed in crucibles.

Even as the disciples of the first century, Christians today can be sure that they will experience times of trial and suffering. Nowhere in the Bible are we told that the Christian life is free from troubles.

But often when periods of testing overtake us, our natural reaction is to ask Why? Why is this happening to me? Unfortunately, if no immediate answer is found we become perplexed. Often these periods of difficulty immobilize us.

THE PURPOSE OF TRIALS

In the first chapter of his letter, the apostle James tells us that God has a purpose in the trials of life we experience. In fact, James shares an exciting secret. These periods of testing can be instruments for our advancement in spiritual growth.

Someone has said, "A Christian is like a teabag, he's not worth much until he's been through some hot water." What James is saying in chapter 1 of his epistle is this—pressure produces! Yes, God has a definite purpose in allowing times of difficulty.

Always remember, it is the fiery pressure of the furnace that produces the hardened steel. It takes the tremendous heat and pressure of the earth's elements to create the precious and costly diamond. It is the crushed flower that produces the perfume. Yes, my friend, pressure produces! There is a purpose in testing. There is a reason behind every trial.

A. B. Simpson wrote,

> Out of the presses of pain
> Cometh the soul's best wine;
> The eyes that have shed no rain
> Can shed but little shine.
>
> *Streams in the Desert*

And because there is a purpose in trials, James prescribes an uncommon way of looking at the common problems of life. "Count it all joy," James says, "when ye fall into divers temptations" (Ja 1:2). The word *divers* that James uses could better be translated "various." Be joyful when you find yourself surrounded by various trials.

Notice that the apostle used the word *when* instead of *if* to indicate the time for joy, "*when* you fall into various trials" (italics added). Times of turmoil and testing are just as much a part of our lives as they were of those first century Christians to whom James was writing. No one is excused from temptation. Competition in school, deadlines in the office, even our day-to-day experiences at home provide us with a multitude of testings. And James says we are to be happy when we find ourselves in the middle of difficulty.

That sounds like strange advice. The natural human reaction is to rejoice when we have *escaped* a particular problem. It is a normal response to run and shrink from the pressures that face us.

But it all depends on how you see the trouble that comes your way. James knew this. He knew that God *does* have a purpose for the problems that face each one of us.

I think of a young boy sailing a small sailboat. One day the string snapped and his boat was blown farther out on the water. An older boy picked up some stones and threw them at the boat. This really disturbed the little boy. But shortly he realized that each falling stone had a purpose. Each stone went beyond the last and drove the boat back to shore.

God has a purpose in our trials.

James recommended "thankful joy" rather than "dull resignation." James is not suggesting that we be silly optimists. No, he is recommending the normal attitude and action of the trusting person who is totally surrendered to Jesus Christ. "Count it all joy" is not the trite response of shallow superficiality, but the honest assessment of the trusting soul.

David wrote, "I will bless the Lord *at all times:* his praise shall *continually* be in my mouth" (Ps 34:1). Praise was the pattern of David's life. And yet David faced pressure much greater than most of us will ever see. One of his sons, Adonijah, broke his heart. Another, Absalom, betrayed him. His oldest son, Amnon, committed adultery. Saul hounded him week after week, and yet this man after God's own heart, said, "Rejoice in the LORD, . . . for praise is comely" (Ps 33:1). Trials are common to all—an attitude of praise is all too uncommon.

SOME PRODUCTS OF TRIALS

Why should we rejoice under pressure? Why does James say to be happy in the midst of trials? Because pressure produces! Produces what? James says that we are to rejoice with the assurance that the "trying of [our] faith worketh patience" (Ja 1:3). Faith meets and bears the testing which pressure brings, and the end result is steadfastness. *Pressure produces patience.*

The book of James is often referred to as the "epistle of faith in action." I wonder, my friend, what is *your* faith like? James describes faith as the Christian's most precious possession—that which is to be strengthened and cultivated at any cost. It is the testing of our faith that produces patience.

Patience is a virtue that builds steadfastness. It was described by Philo as "the queen of the virtues." The testing of our faith is that which develops the Christian's staying power.

When James speaks of steadfastness he speaks of consistent living for Jesus Christ. The pressures and trials which God allows each one of us to experience are intended to make us less sporadic, less intermittent, and more dependable in our Christian lives.

The apostle Paul often compared the Christian life to the competition of the athletic arena. The child of God is in the race of life.

"I press toward the mark," said Paul, "for the prize of the high calling of God in Christ Jesus" (Phil 3:14). To become an accomplished athlete one must have patience—patience that is willing to press forward and to bear pain, patience that will not give up when the game gets rough, patience that endures.

Paul urged the church at Rome to be "patient in tribulation" (Ro 12:12). Our patience is increased as we experience the trial of life. "The [testing] of your faith worketh patience," says James. And the reason for patience is found in the next verse: "that ye may be perfect and entire, wanting nothing" (Ja 1:4*b*). The word *perfect* used here can be defined as "full grown." But how do we grow? James tells us that the pressures of life are God's instruments for our full maturity. We need patience so that we may be brought to full growth and maturity as Christians—that we may be complete. *Besides patience, pressure produces completeness.*

Williams translates the verse: "Let your endurance come to its perfect product so that you may be fully developed and perfectly equipped, without any defects." I'm convinced that there are too many defective Christians around today. Too many of us are incomplete and unable to do God's work because of impatience. The psalmist declared, "Rest in the LORD, and wait patiently for Him" (Ps 37:7). Let us not rush God or His plan for our growth.

As we face the pressures and problems of life, let us seek not a *passive* patience, but rather a *positive* enthusiastic co-operation with God's purpose for our lives.

THE SOLUTION TO TRIALS

Yes, my friend, pressure produces patience and complete-ness. Not only is our patience increased, but James also suggests that pressure produces divine wisdom in the life of the believer. "If any of you lack wisdom, let him ask of God," says James.

Wisdom is the great deficiency of man, but unfortunately it often takes a severe problem in our lives before we realize that we need divine wisdom from above.

What is this wisdom to which James refers? In a single word, it is the matter of guidance—how to act as we pass through the trials of life. It is human and natural to rely upon our *own* wisdom and ability. But James says that when you find yourself in the middle of difficulty, when you lack guidance, you should ask of God. When you do not know where to turn, seek God's wisdom. God is the source of all wisdom.

But you ask How does God give us His wisdom? Proverbs 3:6 says, "In all thy ways acknowledge him, and he shall direct thy paths." Yes, my friend, God will show you His will. God does have a plan for your life. And as you seek *His* wisdom He will direct your path.

Many people today are running here and there looking for the answers to their problems. In their ignorance they ex-periment with alcohol or drugs, they dabble in the occult. They look everywhere for wisdom except in the right place. Eve, in her desire to be wise, went to the tree of the knowledge of good and evil. She sought wisdom from the serpent. "If any of you lack wisdom, let him ask of God" (Ja 1:5). *God* is the source. When you are discouraged, when you're facing a decision, ask God. "Ask God," and the promise is, "it shall be given."

How does God give? He gives "to all men liberally, and upbraideth not" (Ja 1:5). The Greek word translated "liberally" literally means that God gives without conditions—without question as to whether we deserve His gift. The psalmist wrote, "Thou anointest my head with oil; my cup runneth over" (Ps 23:5). God is generous. The cross is the sign of addition.

I'm so glad that God does not give to us, His children, in the same way we give to one another. God has no ulterior motive. He does not question us or chide us. He has no idea of return. God gives to all, even as the apostle Paul said, "life, and breath, and all things" (Ac 17:25). He is the very sustainer of the universe. God has provision for our every need. "If any of you lack wisdom," said James, "let him ask of God."

As we find ourselves engulfed with the trials and testings of life we *can* rejoice. We *can* actually be happy that God is at work in our lives. We *can* be thankful for the patience and wisdom which He gives to us. But we must remember that without faith we will receive nothing. There is a condition attached to the offer of James 1:5—faith.

Faith is the necessary ingredient in all of life. We put money in the bank, and we have faith that it will be rightly used. We get into our automobile and drive down the highway, and we have faith that our brakes will bring us to a stop. We exercise our faith hundreds of times every day. The Bible tells us that patience and wisdom are of tremendous importance, but "without faith it is impossible to please [God]" (Heb 11:6). It is faith that gives us God's power.

When we are in despair, when we are surrounded by trouble we need to look up to God for wisdom, and hook up to God in faith. We must ask of God, but more important we must "ask in faith" (Ja 1:6). Faith is the link that binds our nothingness to His almightiness.

James says we are to "ask in faith, nothing wavering. For he that wavereth is like a wave of the sea driven with the wind and tossed" (Ja 1:6). *Nothing wavering* literally means "without doubting." When everything is going well for us it's easy to have faith without doubting God's Word. The true test comes when we are hit by pressure or pain. James says when you find yourself in the middle of adversity, "ask in faith" and God will meet your need.

Once while Jesus and His disciples were in a boat crossing the Sea of Galilee a great storm came upon them. In Matthew 8 we read that the disciples went to Jesus, "and awoke him, saying, Lord, save us: we perish. And [Jesus] saith unto them, Why are ye fearful, O ye of little faith? Then he arose, and rebuked the winds and the sea; and there was a great calm" (Mt 8:25-26). The disciples had looked at Jesus who was securely sleeping. But *then* they looked at the treacherous waves, and their faith began to waver. They were, as the man James describes, "double minded." They took their eyes off Jesus.

My friend, when the storms of life come down upon you, keep your eyes fixed on Jesus. When the trials become more than you can bear, ask in faith. When everyone around you is sinking, look up and hook up—"ask in faith." Jesus alone can sustain you!

James says, "A double minded man is unstable in all his ways" (Ja 1:8). The child of God cannot be facing two ways at once. We either put our trust in God or we put our trust in ourselves. We must be anchored in the rock of salvation, or we will flounder on the rocks of despair.

The great theologian, John Calvin, was weak and sickly and hounded by persecution; and yet he brilliantly guided thousands of believers during the Reformation. Suffering from rheumatism and migraine headaches, he continued to write profusely and preach powerfully, as well as govern the city of Geneva for twenty-five years. Said Calvin, "You must submit to supreme suffering in order to discover the completion of joy."

Perhaps right now you are experiencing a deep trial, you are going through a time of testing.

James reminds us, "When you're tested in different ways, my fellow Christians, consider it a pure joy because you know the testing of your faith stirs up your power to endure" (Ja 1:2-3, Beck).

James says, Be patient, be joyful, and look up to God. We are to ask of God and to ask in faith. And remember that God is making you into the person He wants you to be.

Remember, FAITH plus TRIALS plus PATIENCE equals COMPLETENESS.

- "Knowing this, that the trying of your faith worketh patience" (Ja 1:3).
- Pressure produces!
- As we face the pressures and problems of life, let us seek not a *passive* acquiescence but rather a *positive* enthusiastic cooperation with God's plan for our lives.
- God is generous. The cross is the sign of addition.
- Look up to God for wisdom and hook up to God in faith.
- When the storms of life come down upon you, keep your eyes fixed on Jesus.

Let no man say when he is tempted, I am tempted of God: for God cannot be tempted with evil, neither tempteth he any man:

But every man is tempted, when he is drawn away of his own lust, and enticed.

Then when lust hath conceived, it bringeth forth sin: and sin, when it is finished, bringeth forth death.

Do not err, my beloved brethren.

Every good gift and every perfect gift is from above, and cometh down from the Father of lights, with whom is no variableness, neither shadow of turning.

JAMES 1:13-17

2

Temptation: Victim or Victor?

JAMES 1:13-17

Oscar Wilde, the well-known British writer, summed up the attitude of millions of people when he said, "I can resist anything except temptation."

Unfortunately "resisting temptation" has gone out of style and "doing what comes naturally" has become the "in" thing.

Once Jesus told His disciples to "Watch and pray, that ye enter not into temptation" (Mt 26:41). What is temptation? Can a person really resist it?

Ever since Eve's battle with Satan in the Garden of Eden, mankind has been tempted to submit to evil.

Like the rain, temptation comes to the just and the unjust alike. Every day thousands of people are injured by what they had considered improbable if not impossible temptations. Someone has said, "They who think they cannot wander will be the first to lose their way."

The convicted embezzler never dreamed that the temptation of greed would one day overcome him and lead him to the prison cell. The loving husband and father, that ideal wife and mother would have laughed in unbelief if told that they would yield to the lust that eventually destroyed their marriage and home.

History tells us of the effects of temptation in the lives of some of the world's most powerful people. As a young student at the Lyons Academy, Napoleon wrote an essay on the dangers of ambition. In his later years, it was ambition and greed that ruined him. As he signed his first death warrant, the Roman emperor, Nero, lamented, "Would that this hand had never learned to write."

Temptation confronts not only the worldly but the godly person as well! The Bible gives us many examples of people who took their eyes off Christ and submitted to temptation.

David slew the Philistine giant and enjoyed God's blessing as he reigned over Israel in kingly splendor. But his later life was scarred with the guilt of adultery and murder. Solomon knelt on the hillside of Gibeon and asked God for wisdom. Yet later in his life he gave in to strange women and heathen deities.

When Peter was told that he would betray Christ, he ardently protested that he would rather die than do such a terrible thing. And yet, just a short while later, he denied that he had ever known his Saviour and Lord.

The Bible states in 1 Corinthians 10:12, "Let him that thinketh he standeth take heed lest he fall." My friend, temptation strikes us at our weakest moment. And yet every temptation is an opportunity for us to draw nearer to God.

MEETING THE TEST

In the first chapter of James we find the word *temptation* is used in two different ways. In verse 12 the word *temptation* refers to a test, a trial, or sorrow.

"Blessed is the man," says James, "that endureth temptation: for when he is tried, he shall receive the crown of life, which the Lord hath promised to them that love him" (Ja 1:12).

Here James is speaking of the trials of life which we all face—times of testing strengthen our faith and demonstrate our Christian maturity. As we saw in chapter 1, these trials serve a particular purpose. They are God's instruments in bringing about spiritual growth and maturity in the life of the believer.

When the Bible says "God tempted Abraham" it means God "tested Abraham's faith" even as the goldsmith commits gold to intense fire to reveal its true character.

When the air force introduces a new jet aircraft they test it, not to destroy it but to demonstrate it. They have every confidence that the airplane will endure the vigorous testing which they give it. This is exactly what James means when he writes: "Blessed is the man that endureth testings." God tests us to display our faith, not to destroy us. It is this trying and testing of our faith that develops patience, that makes us more comformable to the image of Jesus Christ.

Our Lord knew what it was to be tempted. No one knew better the power of Satan in bringing temptations before us. Three times in the wilderness our Lord rebuked the devil and gained victory over temptation. The Scripture tells us that Jesus, "was in all points tempted like as we are, yet without sin" (Heb 4:15).

Jesus Christ was tried and tempted. He experienced great sorrow and suffering, yet He never succumbed to the temptations. This is God's plan for each one of His children.

James writes, "Blessed is the man that endureth temptation: for when he is tried he shall receive the crown of life" (Ja 1:12). The word *tried* is an important word. It is the Greek word which means "to be approved." The picture is of the refiner purifying metal. The impurities must be removed before the metal is "approved." When the refiner can see his own image reflected in the liquid gold, he knows the metal is pure.

All of life is a test—sometimes we are tested by sickness, conflicts, even by death. One of the purposes of these trials of life is that we might be strengthened—that all of the waste of our lives might be removed—so that we might reflect the image of Jesus Christ. Paul the apostle states God's design for every believer. "For whom he did foreknow, he also did predestinate to conform to the image of his Son" (Ro 8:29).

Often these testings we read about in verse 12 are very difficult to bear. Sometimes it seems as if we will break under the heavy load. But James says, "Blessed is the person who endures . . . for he shall receive the crown of life."

This "crown of life" is not some reward that we create or produce of ourselves. James was not referring to a corruptible, earthly crown such as was given to the winner of an athletic contest. He was, rather, suggesting that the Christian who stands the test and remains true despite all circumstances, will receive the crown which *is* life. Jesus said, "I am come that they might have life and that they might have it more abundantly" (Jn 10:10). This crown of life is for those who overcome and for those alone.

Remember that *pressure produces perseverance and ultimately a crown.*

Do not blame God

In James 1:13 we find the word *tempted* used in an entirely different way. As we have seen, the word *temptation* in verse 12 refers to a test or trial. Here in verse 13 the word *tempted* indicates the "solicitation to do evil."

James says, "Let no man say when he is tempted, I am tempted of God: for God cannot be tempted with evil, neither tempteth he any man" (Ja 1:13). Although Satan sought to tempt Jesus Christ with all his trickery, there was absolutely nothing in the nature of Christ that responded to evil.

Speaking of Jehovah, the prophet Habakkuk declares, "Thou art of purer eyes than to behold evil, and canst not look on iniquity" (Hab 1:13). God cannot tempt us with evil, since evil is completely contrary to all that He is.

In James 1:17 we read that God is the giver of every good and perfect gift. God is all *goodness*. He is all *perfection*. James continues by saying that every good gift, "is from above, and cometh down from the Father of lights, with whom is no variableness, neither shadow of turning." God is good, God is perfect, and God is unchangeable!

My friend, are you blaming God for your failures and sins? Blaming God is not new. Even Adam blamed God for his disobedience, "The woman whom *thou* gavest to be with me, she gave me of the tree, and I did eat" (Gen 3:12, italics added). Adam may have been the first, but he certainly wasn't the last man to hide behind the skirts of a woman. Adam blamed both the woman *and* God. He really said God gave me this woman so ultimately God is responsible for my sin. May God deliver us from excuses!

We see in Genesis 3:13 that Eve was not one bit better. When the Lord questioned her as to what she had done she answered, "The serpent beguiled me, and I did eat." She blamed the serpent for her sin.

My friend, are you blaming someone else today for the sin in your life?

A man once told me, "I can't help it that I'm so weak; my environment is bad. My parents were careless—I inherited my passions." It's always easy to blame our environment or heredity. But in a sense this is blaming God for our failure.

Several days after the senseless and tragic assassination of President Kennedy I was in a barber shop having my hair cut. In the course of our conversation about the tragedy the barber carelessly said, "Why did *God* do it?" I quickly answered, "God didn't do it. Lee Harvey Oswald did it." This man was blaming God for the horrible crime of a confused, desperate, godless man.

Make no mistake! God never tempts any man with evil! James said, "Let no man say . . . I am tempted of God: for God cannot be tempted with evil, neither tempteth he any man" (Ja 1:13).

Just because God allows us to experience trials and testings does not mean that He also tempts us to do evil. God by His very nature, says James, "cannot be tempted with evil" (v. 13). God hates sin. He cannot stand to look upon it, and He is incapable of influencing us to become involved in it.

It is true that while the Bible says that God sometimes blinds men's hearts and gives them up to a reprobate mind, it is also true, as the apostle Paul declares, that God's action is the result of "the lusts of their own hearts" (Ro 1:24b). God is not in the business of tempting men to do evil.

"But," James continues, "every man is tempted [or enticed], when he is drawn away of his own lust" (Ja 1:14). When he is "drawn away." The picture here is of a fisherman beguiling a fish from under the rocks. The hungry fish takes the bait and is caught on the hook. So it is with us. We are drawn out, tempted, and enticed by our own lust and desires. In reality we are snared by our own bait.

Desires are not evil in and of themselves. Even as the fish's hunger for food is natural, we have natural and normal desires. But many things which in themselves may be harmless become deadly when joined with another ingredient. Carbon, for instance, is needful and good. So is oxygen. But carbon and oxygen together form carbon monoxide—a deadly gas.

Temptation is the invitation to do wrong! *Sin* is the voluntary action of doing wrong! It is not sinful to be tempted, but it is sinful to yield to evil temptation.

THERE IS A WAY OUT

Is there a way out? Are we destined to be victims of our

sinful natures, or can we be victors? What a thrill it is to know that victory is absolutely possible! It is available to all.

To be victorious you must first submit your life to Jesus Christ and receive Him as Saviour. Someone has said, "If you would master temptation, you must first let Christ master you."

Mankind is like a clock whose mainspring is broken. He needs to be totally renewed on the inside, but the repairs must be supplied from without. He cannot save himself. Even so, men and women today need someone to remake them. That someone is Jesus Christ, the Redeemer of man's soul and nature. He loves you. He died for you, and He wants you to turn to Him in repentance and faith.

Salvation is the first step to victory over temptation.

Second, to the believer—the child of God—is given the privilege of prayer in overcoming temptation. James says, "If any [man] lack wisdom, let him ask of God, that giveth to all men [generously]" (Ja 1:5).

Do you need help in overcoming your weakness? Ask God! Do you need deliverance from the power and temptation of sin? Ask God! He alone is able to deliver you. Often I have cried out, "Lord help me," and God's deliverance was given.

God's Word proclaims that "There hath no temptation taken you but such as is common to man: but God is faithful, who will not suffer you to be tempted above that ye are able; but will with the temptation also make a way of escape, that ye may be able to bear it" (1 Co 10:13).

D. L. Moody once said, "When Christians find themselves exposed to temptation they should pray to God to uphold them, and when they are tempted they should not be discouraged. It is not a sin to be tempted; the sin is to fall into temptation."

Third, apply the Word of God. Jesus put Satan to flight

by quoting Scripture. Jesus said, "It is written," and so must we fortify ourselves with the Word of God.

Fourth, submit to the indwelling Holy Spirit. When a drop of water falls on a hot stove, the water never really touches the stove. It rests on a thin cushion of very hot air. Heat overcomes gravity and holds the water away until it evaporates. To the child of God, who is directed by the Holy Spirit, temptation may come but it will not be able to destroy us. For God has promised, "Greater is he that is in you, than he that is in the world" (1 Jn 4:4).

In your hour of trial, remember God is faithful. He knows your capacity. He will give you all the strength you need to overcome temptation, or He will make a way of deliverance for you.

- "Let no man say when he is tempted, I am tempted of God: for God cannot be tempted with evil, neither tempteth he any man" (Ja 1:13).
- God tests us to display our faith, not to destroy us.
- May God deliver us from excuses!
- It is not sinful to be tempted, but it is sinful to yield to evil temptation.
- "If you would master temptation, you must first let Jesus Christ master you."
- Jesus answered Satan, "It is written," and so must we fortify ourselves with the Word of God.
- We must submit ourselves to the indwelling Holy Spirit because "Greater is he that is in you, than he that is in the world" (1 Jn 4:4).

Wherefore, my beloved brethren, let every man be swift to hear, slow to speak, slow to wrath:

For the wrath of man worketh not the righteousness of God.

Wherefore lay apart all filthiness and superfluity of naughtiness, and receive with meekness the engrafted word, which is able to save your souls.

But be ye doers of the word, and not hearers only, deceiving your own selves.

JAMES 1:19-22

3

Practicing God's Word

JAMES 1:19-22

There are no more worlds to conquer!

That was the cry of Alexander the Great after he and his Grecian armies swept across the then known world. Alexander was one of the few men in history who deserved to be called "great." He was energetic, versatile, and intelligent. He was bold and impulsive; and he was strong in his loves and loyalties.

Hatred was not generally a part of Alexander's nature. However, several times in his life he was tragically defeated by anger. On one of those occasions, Cletus, a dear friend of Alexander and general in his army, became intoxicated and began to ridicule the emperor in front of his men. Blinded by anger, quick as lightning, Alexander snatched a spear from the hand of a soldier and hurled it at Cletus. Although he had only intended to scare the drunken general, his aim was true and the spear took the life of his childhood friend.

Deep remorse followed his anger. Overcome with guilt, Alexander attempted to take his own life with the same spear, but he was stopped by his men. For days he lay sick calling for his friend, Cletus, chiding himself as a murderer.

Alexander the Great conquered many cities, he conquered many countries, but he had failed miserably to conquer his own spirit.

Throughout history there have been many men and women whose lives have been destroyed by pride and passion. Many, like Alexander the Great, have been beaten in their prime because they lacked self-control. Here in the book of James we find the solution to this conflict. In the first chapter of his epistle, James tells us how to control our passions. He demonstrates our need to practice the Word of God.

In verse 19 James says, "Let every man be swift to hear, slow to speak, slow to wrath."

BE SWIFT TO HEAR

Psychotherapists tell us that listening is probably the most simple and effective technique for helping troubled people. Listening has been described as an art that requires as much time, effort, and perseverance as any other art form.

Poor listening is responsible for a tremendous waste in education and industry. Many other areas of life are affected by poor listening. Thousands of marriages are ended each year because the husband and wife stopped listening to each other! Much of the talked-about generation gap is the result of parents and children who fail to listen to one another.

Oftentimes, we are so interested in getting out our next sentence, we don't even hear the one with whom we are speaking. In reality, the way you listen to others reveals whether you yourself should be listened to.

Many people, it seems, suffer from this disease of poor attention. Some will miss heaven and eternal life because they did not listen. Others will miss being used by God because they failed to be attentive to His voice.

In the book of the Acts the apostle Paul spoke of those people of Rome who were poor listeners. Their ears were closed to the gospel of Jesus Christ. "For the heart of this people is waxed gross, and their ears are dull of hearing, and their eyes have they closed; lest they should see with their eyes, and hear with their ears, and understand with their heart, and should be converted" (Ac 28:27). These people refused to listen to the Word of God! They were dull of hearing.

James said, "Be swift to hear." Swift to hear what? Swift to hear the Word of God. The first step in salvation is hearing. The Bible tells us that "faith cometh by hearing, and hearing by the Word of God" (Ro 10:17). We are to be "swift to hear" the Word of God.

Paul wrote to Timothy, his son in the faith, of the value in "listening" to God's Word. "From a child thou hast known the holy scriptures, which are able to make thee wise unto salvation through faith which is in Christ Jesus. All scripture is given by inspiration of God, and is profitable for doctrine, for reproof, for correction, for instruction in righteousness: that the man of God may be perfect, throughly furnished unto all good works" (2 Ti 3:15-17).

Moffatt translates these words, "quick to listen." Are you a good listener? Are you really hearing what God has to say? As men and women tune their hearts and minds to the signal of God's Word the Holy Spirit enables them to "hear" the voice of God.

They begin to realize their sinful nature. They see their need of a Saviour, and they are convicted by what they hear. The Bible becomes a spiritual hearing aid.

In the parable of the sower, our Lord likened the seed which fell on good ground to the man that "*heareth* the word, and understandeth it; which also beareth fruit" (Mt 13:23, italics added).

It is very sad when men and women fail to listen to one another. But it is eternally fatal when they fail to listen to God. Jesus said, "My brethren are these which hear the word of God, and do it" (Lk 8:21).

James said, "Be swift to hear." How is *your* hearing, my friend? Are you practicing the Word of God?

BE SLOW TO SPEAK

There is no mistake in the order of command given by James. It stands to reason that if we are truly "swift to hear" we will then be "slow to speak" (Ja 1:19). James, of course, is not suggesting that we be slow in talking, but rather slow *to* talk.

It seems as though everybody today has something to say. Never before in history have so many said so much and accomplished so little! This is an age of talkers.

The ancient philosopher, Zeno, once said, "We have two ears and one mouth; therefore we should listen twice as much as we speak." That's good advice!

A young man known for his incessant talking once came to Socrates for speech lessons. "I will teach you," said Socrates, "but I will have to charge you double my fee. First I have to teach you how to hold your tongue, and then how to use it."

Unfortunately, some people shift their minds into neutral and tramp down the gas pedal of wild talk. Their tongues become, as the discarded match in the forest, a whirlwind of fire and destruction.

James says, "Be slow to speak," weigh your words. Don't talk before you listen.

A poet has penned:

> "The boneless tongue so small and weak
> can crash and kill," declared the Greek.
> "The tongue destroys a greater horde,"
> the Turks assert, "than does the Sword!"

Solomon wrote, "Whoever keeps his mouth and his tongue keepeth his soul from troubles" (Pro 21:23).

Contentious tongues have hindered the work of God a thousand times over. Critical tongues have closed church doors. Careless tongues have broken the hearts and homes of many of God's choice servants. The sins of the tongue have dirtied the pure white gown of the bride of Christ.

James obviously is referring here to the problems which had already been caused by the casual use of the tongue of some teachers in the church. These "creators of controversy" were, by their troublesome talk, doing more harm than good. They were tearing down rather than building up the body of Christ.

The untamed tongue is, as James declares, "an unruly evil, full of deadly poison" (Ja 3:8). Yes, my friend, we need to be swift to hear and slow to speak.

"Wherefore," said the apostle Peter, "laying aside all malice, and all guile, and hypocrisies, and envies, and all evil speakings, as newborn babes desire the [pure] milk of the word [of God], that ye may grow" (1 Pe 2:1-2).

We need to practice the Word of God!

BE SLOW TO WRATH

The third element of James' command is closely connected to the first and second. "Be swift to hear, slow to speak," and third, "slow to wrath." There is a definite relationship between speech and anger. R. V. G. Tasker suggests that "an essential condition of listening to God is that the mind should not be distracted by thoughts of resentment, ill-temper, hatred or vengeance, all of which are comprised in the general term *the wrath of man.*"

Anger inflames words which are spoken in haste. And the more one talks the angrier he becomes. We need hot hearts, but we do not need hot heads. James says that if we would truly practice the Word of God we must possess a quick ear, a cautious tongue, and a calm temper.

In Proverbs 16:32 we read "He that is slow to anger is better than the mighty; and he that ruleth his spirit than he that taketh a city." A friend said to me, "I lose my temper, but it's all over in a minute." Yes, so is an atomic bomb. But what about the destruction that is wrought.

Do you rule your spirit? Or do you become easily inflamed? Again in Proverbs we are told that "a soft answer turneth away wrath: but grievous words stir up anger" (Pro 15:1). May Jesus Christ teach us the power of a soft answer.

Why should we be slow to wrath or anger? Well, James continues in verse 20, "For the wrath of man worketh not the righteousness of God." Man's anger hinders God's work. When you lose your temper—you really lose something. You lose the ability to think sanely and to make balanced decisions. Temper clouds the mind. It confuses our judgment and creates unhappiness. It spoils our love for other people.

Anger borders on insanity. When we are angry, we say irrational things. We need to exercise care in our discussions, even when we discuss the Scriptures.

Paul, in his letter of instruction to Timothy, warned of this. "Again I say," said Paul, "don't get involved in foolish arguments which only upset people and make them angry. God's people must not be quarrelsome; they must be gentle, patient teachers of those who are wrong. Be humble when you are trying to teach those who are mixed up concerning the truth. For if you talk meekly and courteously to them, they are more likely, with God's help, to turn away from their wrong ideas and believe what is true" (2 Ti 2:23-25, Living Bible).

Paul instructs that a person in a place of spiritual leadership should be one "not soon angry" (Titus 1:7). Remember, we must be angry with sin but not with the sinner.

Is anger ever right? Is there ever a time when we *should* be angry? The answer is yes!

On one occasion Jesus took a whip and drove the buyers and sellers out of the temple. Overturning their money tables, He declared that they had made His house a "den of thieves" (Mt 21:13). It was our Lord's love for His Father and His glory that issued forth in righteous indignation.

Another time Jesus was harshly criticized by the religious leaders for healing a man on the Sabbath day. Mark's gospel tells us that afterward He looked "on them with anger, being grieved for the hardness of their hearts" (Mk 3:5). He looked on them with anger, not a revengeful anger, but that of compassion. Jesus' anger was not self-serving. Martin Luther claimed that he "never did anything well until his righteous wrath was excited, and then he could do anything well."

The basic cause of *our* anger is most often egotism and selfishness. We don't think of it in this way. We make excuses for our quick temper—our nationality, our heredity, or even the color of our hair. But in reality our anger is the bad fruit of selfishness. And as James declares, "It worketh not the righteousness of God." Holy wrath is free from selfishness.

Yes, my friend, we are to be "slow to wrath." Our tongues, our nature, our total personality must be committed to Jesus Christ.

Paul said, "I am crucified with Christ: nevertheless I live; yet not I, but Christ liveth in me: and the life which I now live in the flesh I live by the faith of the Son of God, who loved me, and gave himself for me" (Gal 2:20).

It is Christ *in* me, living His life *through* me. No man can tame the tongue—but I have good news, Jesus can.

James admonished believers to "be swift to hear, slow to speak, slow to wrath." How do we do this? What is the secret of a life free from the pitfalls of sin?

There is an answer. There is a way out. James declares that we are to practice the Word of God in our lives. "Wherefore," says James, "putting away all filthiness and overflowing of wickedness, receive with the meekness the implanted word, which is able to save your souls" (Ja 1:21, ERV). What is the way of escape? We are to put off all wickedness and receive the Word of God which delivers us.

The writer of Hebrews prescribes this same remedy. "Wherefore seeing we also are compassed about with so great a cloud of witnesses, let us lay aside every weight, and the sin which doth so easily beset us, and let us run with patience the race that is set before us" (Heb 12:1). A runner who wants to be a winner must first strip away all the excess clothing that would weigh him down and hold him back. God's Word is the instrument to deliver us from the insanity of our old nature. We are to lay aside all our sin. We are to put away all our corruption and evilness, and wholeheartedly welcome God's Word into our lives. David said, "Thy word have I hid in mine heart, that I might not sin against thee" (Ps 119:11).

The prophet Jeremiah declared, "Thy words were found, and I did eat them" (Jer 15:16). The psalmist asks, "[How] shall a young man cleanse his way? by taking heed thereto according to thy word" (Ps 119:9).

James says, "Be ye doers of the word, and not hearers only" (Ja 1:22). My friend, are you practicing the Word of God? Jesus said, "If ye love me, keep my commandments" (Jn 14:15). Today Jesus calls upon you to act, to do, and to practice what the Bible says.

- "Therefore whosoever heareth these sayings of mine, and *doeth them,* I will liken him unto a wise man, which built his house upon a rock" (Mt 7:24).
- The way you listen to others reveals whether you yourself should be listened to.

- "We have two ears and one mouth; therefore we should listen twice as much as we speak." ZENO
- When you lose your temper—you really lose something. You lose the ability to think sanely and to make balanced decisions.

But be ye doers of the word, and not hearers only, deceiving your own selves.

For if any be a hearer of the word, and not a doer, he is like unto a man beholding his natural face in a glass:

For he beholdeth himself, and goeth his way, and straightway forgetteth what manner of man he was.

But whoso looketh into the perfect law of liberty, and continueth therein, he being not a forgetful hearer, but a doer of the work, this man shall be blessed in his deed.

If any man among you seem to be religious, and bridleth not his tongue, but deceiveth his own heart, this man's religion is vain.

Pure religion and undefiled before God and the Father is this, To visit the fatherless and widows in their affliction, and to keep himself unspotted from the world.

JAMES 1:22-27

4

Faith That is Real

JAMES 1:22-27

Many things in our world are fake!

Last year alone over twenty-three million dollars in counterfeit money was seized by the United States Secret Service. Nearly 1,800 people were arrested for trying to pass phony bills. Every year thousands of people are convicted of forgery and embezzlement. Con artists have become an ever increasing threat to the unsuspecting person.

In the spring of 1971 the whole world was shocked to read of the giant hoax surrounding billionaire Howard Hughes. Late in March a federal grand jury indicted Clifford Irving and his wife, Edith, on charges of fraud and forgery. The Irvings were accused and later convicted of concocting a fake autobiography of Hughes and selling the manuscript to McGraw-Hill publishers for three-quarters of a million dollars.

Through the use of extensive research into material already published about the billionaire, the Irvings were able to create a phony manuscript good enough to fool the experts.

Criminals, of course, have no monopoly on the world of make-believe. The Bible tells us that there are many counterfeit Christians in our world today. Many people appear to be religious but know nothing of a saving faith. In reality they are nothing more than phonies.

Webster's dictionary defines the word *phony* as that which is "not genuine, spurious, counterfeit, or false." In other words, a phony is a fake!

The word *phony* actually finds its origin in an ancient confidence game in which a brass ring was falsely sold as a ring of gold.

A powerful illustration of this trickery is found in 1 Kings 14. Under Solomon, Israel enjoyed golden days of victory. After he died, his son, Rehoboam, ruled Judah. "And it came to pass in the fifth year of king Rehoboam, that Shishak king of Egypt came up against Jerusalem: and he took away the treasures of the house of the LORD, and the treasures of the king's house; he even took away all: and he took away all the shields of gold which Solomon had made. And king Rehoboam made in their stead brazen shields, and committed them unto the hands of the chief of the guard, which kept the door of the king's house" (1 Ki 14:25-27).

Rehoboam had replaced the golden shields with those made of brass. They were forgeries! They were phony! And they even fooled the guards and the people.

Yes, polished brass looks like gold, but it isn't gold. Today there are many people who look and sound just like Christians, but they are not Christians! They know how to act; they know just the right way to talk; they go through all the motions—but in reality they are phonies!

In the first chapter of his epistle, James attacks that which is false and unreal. He attacks the shallow, hypocritical religion of the phony. James describes faith that is real. He presents true Christianity.

James says that the Word of God is our guide to reality. "But be ye doers of the word, and not hearers only, deceiving your own selves. For if any be a hearer of the word, and not a doer, he is like a man beholding his natural face in a glass: for he beholdeth himself, and goeth his way, and immediately forgetteth what manner of man he was" (Ja 1:22-24).

James tells us that the Bible is a mirror—it shows us what we really are.

Throughout the Scriptures we find similes are used to describe God's Word. A simile is a figure of speech in which two unlike things are compared. Here James uses the simile of the mirror.

Psalm 119 compares the Bible to a lamp. "Thy word is a lamp unto my feet, and a light unto my path" (Ps 119:105). The Bible illuminates! A thousand times I have found light and guidance from God's Word.

The prophet Jeremiah compared the Bible to a fire and hammer. "Is not my word like as a fire? saith the LORD; and like a hammer that breaketh the rock in pieces" (Jer 23:29). My friend, have you ever felt the fire of this book? Have you ever experienced its melting force and its breaking power?

Remember what it is like to hit your thumb with a hammer? Rarely do you get by without a bruise or a blister. God's Word often bruises us like a hammer as it convicts and convinces us of our sin.

The apostle Paul, in writing to the church at Ephesus, speaks of the "washing of water by the word" (Eph 5:26). The Bible washes us!

The writer of Hebrews described the Word of God as "quick, and powerful, and sharper than any twoedged sword, piercing even to the dividing asunder of soul and spirit, and of the joints and marrow, and is a discerner of the thoughts and intents of the heart" (Heb 4:12).

This great book, the Bible, is compared to many things. It is a lamp, a fire, a hammer, water, and a sword.

But here in James chapter 1 the Bible is likened unto a mirror. When James compared the Word of God to a mirror his audience did not think of a shiny glass mirror as we do today. The mirrors of ancient times were made of highly polished metal, mostly brass. It was a mirror such as this that the brilliant Socrates used when instructing his students in public speaking.

There are two basic ways that a person can evaluate his performance—two means of discovering how he looks or appears. He can either look in a mirror and observe himself, or he can use the wonders of photography.

The photographer, of course, can work miracles. He can remove blemishes, he can touch up here and there, he can shade in light spots, and generally make us look pretty good. But the photograph is not always accurate. At times it can be very flattering to us. The photographer deals with us in mercy, not justice.

A mirror, on the other hand, is absolutely just and dependable. It reveals our true image, blemishes and all. It shows us exactly as we are!

When I arise in the morning and walk in front of the mirror, I am immediately confronted with all of the corrective work that needs to be done. If I simply walk away and forget what I see, I am only fooling myself—certainly no one else!

The Bible tells us that "the [human] heart is deceitful above all things, and desperately wicked" (Jer 17:9). The mirror of God's Word points out all our weakness and wickedness. And unless we heed its instruction, unless we make the necessary corrections in our lives, we are only engaging in deluded optimism. We are nothing more than a phony!

Paul said, "I felt fine so long as I did not understand what the law really demanded. But when I learned the truth, I realized that I had broken the law and was a sinner, doomed to die" (Ro 7:9, Living). When Paul saw his sin revealed, he realized that he was condemned before God.

This great and priceless book not only shows us up, it is meant to clean us up. The Bible reveals and cleanses.

Under the sacrificial system of the Old Testament, the

brazen laver in the tabernacle court was to provide cleansing for the priest. In Exodus 38 we find that Bezaleel "made the laver of brass, and the foot of it of brass, of the lookingglasses of the women assembling, which assembled at the door of the tabernacle of the congregation" (Ex 38:8).

How interesting and suggestive! The glass which revealed the need for cleansing led to the fountain of cleansing. The brass laver was made from the looking glasses of the women of that day.

The story is told of an African princess of the last century who lived in the heart of the uncivilized jungle. For years this chieftain's daughter had been told by all that she was the most beautiful woman in the entire tribe. Although she had no mirror to view herself, she had been convinced of her unparalleled beauty.

One day when an exploring party traveled through that part of Africa, the princess was given a mirror as a gift. For the first time in her life she was able to see her own reflection. Her immediate reaction was to smash the mirror on the nearest rock. Why? Because for the first time in her life she knew the truth. What other people had told her all those years was of little importance. What she had believed about herself made no difference. She saw for the first time that her beauty was not genuine. It was false.

The mirror of God's Word works in the exact same way in our lives. Our friends may tell us we are wonderful, and we may even fool ourselves into believing it. We can dream up thousands of ways of improving our own self-image, but when we read the Word of God we see ourselves exactly as we are! It is impossible to be indifferent to the Bible. You may hear it and choose to do nothing about it, but the Bible will do something to you. Truth heard and ignored is dangerous.

On one occasion Jesus was teaching in the temple when a

group of scribes and Pharisees came to Him with a woman
that had been caught in the act of adultery. Jesus, knowing
their hearts and motives, said unto them, "He that is without
sin among you, let him first cast a stone at her" (Jn 8:7b).
John records that when they heard those words, "being convicted by their own conscience, went out one by one, beginning at the eldest, even unto the last: and Jesus was left
alone, and the woman standing in the midst" (Jn 8:9).

These religious leaders heard the words of Jesus, and they
were convicted. They recognized their guilt, but they did
nothing about it. They were hearers only.

James said that if our religion is true we must be "doers
of the word." We must act upon what we know to be true.
We must make the necessary changes in our lives and we
must "conform to the perfect law of [God's] liberty."

My friend, the Bible is our guide to reality. It is our blueprint for holy living. Jesus said, "My brethren are these
which hear the word of God, and do it" (Lk 8:21). True religion demands complete obedience to God's Word.

Not only do we have a guide to true religion, but in James
1:26-27 we are given a *test* of true religion.

James says, "If any man among you seem to be religious,
and bridleth not his tongue, but deceiveth his own heart, this
man's religion is vain. Pure religion and undefiled before
God and the Father is this, To visit the fatherless and widows
in their affliction, and to keep himself unspotted from the
world" (Ja 1:26-27).

A BRIDLED TONGUE

The first test of real salvation is a spirit-controlled tongue.

Moses was a great servant of Jehovah, but at times he suffered from an uncontrolled tongue. When the children of
Israel's water supply was depleted, they accused Moses of
leading them into the desert to die. Unable to control his

temper, Moses smote the rock and shouted, "Hear now, ye rebels; must we bring water out of this rock?" (Num 20:10). God was faithful and He satisfied the people, but Moses was barred from entering the promised land.

Or consider the apostle John. Gentle John was probably as close to Jesus as any other person. He is called "the disciple that Jesus loved," and yet he too experienced tongue trouble. Luke's gospel tells how friends of Jesus had tried to arrange lodging for Him in Samaria. When the Samaritans would not receive Jesus, James and John exploded and said, "Lord, wilt thou that we command fire to come down from heaven, and consume them?" (Lk 9:54). But we read that Jesus rebuked them and said, "The Son of man is not come to destroy men's lives, but to save them" (Lk 9:56).

Loving John was usually Mr. Reliable. More than once he had kept the apostolic band from impulsive conduct, but here his tongue ran wild.

It has been said that the control of the tongue is the barometer of Christian maturity. The test of reality with God is not a man's ability to speak his mind, but to bridle his tongue. Paul told the Ephesians to "let no corrupt communication proceed out of your mouth" (Eph 4:29). The test of true religion, the indication of a genuine salvation, is the control of the tongue. If a man cannot do this, says James, his "religion is vain." It is nothing more than a sham or fake. The man with the uncontrolled tongue is a stumbling block to those who judge true religion by him.

AN UNDERSTANDING HEART

From the negative aspect of an uncontrolled tongue James proceeds to the positive aspect of "true religion" in action. Real salvation, says James, is demonstrated by an understanding heart. "Pure religion and undefiled before God and the Father is this, to visit the fatherless and widows in their affliction, and to keep himself unspotted from the world" (Ja 1:27).

In this verse, James has not given us a complete definition of salvation. Neither is he offering a blueprint for social action. But rather, James is suggesting an illustration of a faith that is genuine. He is saying, "If there is any substance to your convictions, if there is any reality in your faith, you will show a love and concern for those who are in need." This truly is faith in action!

My friend, when was the last time you visited a needy family—not just to say a brief hello, but to provide tangible help and assistance? The cry of the widows and orphans was heard by Jesus, and we must hear them too.

The word *visit* which James uses here is the same word which describes the mystery of the incarnation, the birth of Jesus Christ. Our great God "visited" this poor and confused world in the flesh—through the person of Jesus Christ. He came to us in all of our poverty. Now we are to visit the needy of our world.

A SANCTIFIED LIFE

Finally, if we are "doers of the word," if we possess a genuine faith, if our religion is true, the result will be a sanctified life. James says, "Pure religion . . . is this . . . to keep [ourselves] unspotted from the world" (Ja 1:27), or as Moffatt translates this, "from the stain of the world."

I once saw a sign in a department store which read, "slightly soiled, greatly reduced in value." The Christian whose life has been soiled and dirtied by the stains of sin becomes of little value. His effectiveness for Jesus Christ is greatly reduced.

What a high calling to live a spotless life in this world.

Jesus was offered as a lamb without spot. The Scriptures tell us that Christ will someday present His church without spot or blemish as a glorious bride. A real Christian is a clean Christian. This is what true religion is all about.

Paul told believers not to be "conformed to this world," but to be "transformed by the renewing of your mind" (Ro 12:2). J. B. Phillips translates this, "Don't let the world squeeze you into its own mould." Throughout the Word of God the call for moral purity goes out to all who name the name of Jesus Christ.

The big question is What is true religion? How can we be genuine? The answer is: by daily receiving the Word of God which delivers our souls; by controlling our tongues and speaking the truth in love; by cultivating a sincere interest and genuine concern for those in need; by keeping our lives unspotted from the world; and by abstaining from the very appearances of evil.

My friend, is your faith true or false? Are you real or are you a phony? Is your experience gold or brass? Today you can seek cleansing and begin to live a life that is pleasing to God. First John 1:9 states, "If we confess our sins, he is faithful and just to forgive us our sins, and to cleanse us from all unrighteousness."

———————

- "Pure religion and undefiled before God and the Father is this, To visit the fatherless and widows in their affliction, and to keep himself unspotted from the world" (Ja 1:27).
- A phony is a fake!
- The mirror of God's Word points out all our weakness and wickedness. And unless we heed its instruction, unless we make the necessary corrections in our lives, we are only engaging in deluded optimism.
- The Christian whose life has been soiled . . . [will find that] his effectiveness for Jesus Christ is greatly reduced.

My brethren, have not the faith of our Lord Jesus Christ, the Lord of glory, with respect of persons.

For if there come unto your assembly a man with a gold ring, in goodly apparel, and there come in also a poor man in vile raiment;

And ye have respect to him that weareth the gay clothing, and say unto him, Sit thou here in a good place; and say to the poor, Stand thou there, or sit here under my footstool:

Are ye not then partial in yourselves, and are become judges of evil thoughts?

Hearken, my beloved brethren, Hath not God chosen the poor of this world rich in faith, and heirs of the kingdom which he hath promised to them that love him?

But ye have despised the poor. Do not rich men oppress you, and draw you before the judgment seats?

Do not they blaspheme that worthy name by the which ye are called?

If ye fulfil the royal law according to the scripture, Thou shalt love thy neighbour as thyself, ye do well:

But if ye have respect to persons, ye commit sin, and are convinced of the law as transgressors.

JAMES 2:1-9

5

The Peril of Prejudice

JAMES 2:1-9

"Prejudice," said Mark Twain, "is the ink with which all history is written."

Unfortunately there is much truth to be found in those words. Prejudice and discrimination of every kind have shaped the course of human events down through the centuries. Many of the world's greatest conflicts have been a direct result of the prejudiced thinking of mankind. And prejudice remains rampant in the world today! Everywhere we look, in every corner of the world, we see the turmoil caused by the discrimination of one group of people by another.

In his book entitled *The Roots of Prejudice*, Arnold Rose suggests that prejudice almost always involves the "mistreatment of people without their having done anything to merit such mistreatment. It has been a source of human unhappiness and misunderstanding wherever and whenever it has arisen."

Prejudice, of course, is not new. It has existed in most parts of the world in every period of history. During the past three centuries many Americans have been guilty of showing racial prejudice toward men of red, black, and yellow skin. In other parts of our world, discrimination has been expressed toward the white man in much the same way.

But the color of skin is not always the basis for prejudice and discrimination. Much of the trouble facing our world today is the result of people expressing religious, economic, and political prejudice toward one another.

In Jesus' day the Jews detested the Samaritans. The "half-breeds" from Samaria were looked upon as a godless and inferior people. A good Jew would journey many miles out of his way just so that he would not have to set foot inside Samaria.

From an earlier time the Egyptians hated the Jews. On several occasions they had even attempted mass extermination of the people of Israel. You'll remember the story of baby Moses, how his mother hid him in a basket so that he would be delivered from the death sentence Pharaoh had placed upon all Jewish baby boys.

Throughout Scripture we are told of men who were guilty of prejudice. Jonah was a prejudiced Jew who refused to obey God's command to take His message to the city of Nineveh. He was full of bigotry and hate toward the Gentile Assyrians. The apostle Peter also had to be confronted by God in a dream before he was willing to preach the gospel to the Gentiles of Caesarea.

Regardless of the background, motive, or cause, God's Word emphatically declares that all prejudice is sin. Luke tells us that after Peter was shown the error of his way, he "opened his mouth, and said, Of a truth I perceive that God is no respecter of persons: but in every nation he that feareth him, and worketh righteousness, is accepted with him" (Ac 10:34-35). God is color-blind to skin.

You see, with God, prejudice makes no sense! Paul refuted the idea of racial superiority by declaring to the intellectuals of Athens that God "hath made of one blood all nations of men for to dwell on all the face of the earth, and hath determined the times before appointed, and the bounds of their habitation" (Ac 17:26).

God is the Creator of the universe! He loves all of His creation, and He is no respector of persons.

In the second chapter of this epistle, James gives us an excellent example of the evilness of prejudice. Within the early church there were many more "poor" Christians than there were "rich" ones. For the most part, the wealthy Jews of that day held nothing but contempt for those who were followers of "the carpenter's son."

And so it appears that some people in the church did not know how to treat a man of means. James pictures two men arriving to worship. One man wore a gold ring, goodly apparel, and flashy clothing. The other, obviously poor, arrived in shabby dress. The shortsighted usher who greeted the two quickly showed his feelings by the way in which he seated each man. He placed the well-dressed worshiper in an excellent seat, and the poor man he told to sit on the floor or stand up! He obviously was attempting to impress the rich man and win his favor, while at the same time he was showing no concern whatsoever for the man in shabby clothing.

In other words, the usher was guilty of prejudice. Undoubtedly he had made class distinctions in his mind before he even got into this spot.

And yet, as we read the Word of God we find that this type of attitude, or for that matter, any act of prejudice, is totally inconsistent with the grace of God and has no place in the life of the believer.

RESPECT OF PERSONS IS INCONSISTENT WITH GOD'S GRACE

In refuting the behavior of the nearsighted usher, James declares, "Hearken, my beloved brethren, Hath not God chosen the poor of this world rich in faith, and heirs of the

kingdom which he hath promised to them that love him?"
(Ja 2:5).

God in His grace often chooses "the poor of this world."
The message of the birth of Jesus was first revealed to the
poor, humble shepherds. God did not choose to send a special messenger to inform those of royalty that His Son would
come to earth. He instead declared that message of good
tidings to lowly shepherds—"The poor of this world."

And consider the One who came to this earth. Jesus Christ
was born into the most humble setting—a manger, a feeding
place for animals. He came from a poor home. He worked
with His hands as a carpenter. He Himself declared that He
had "not where to lay his head" (Mt 8:20).

Yes, my friend, Jesus Christ often identified with the "poor
of this world." He knew the problems and needs of the un-
derprivileged and the oppressed. Luke says that Jesus came
"to preach [good tidings] to the poor" (Lk 4:18). Throughout His entire earthly ministry He ministered to the downtrodden and needy.

Some people seem to think that God's love is only for the
educated and well-to-do. Like the ignorant usher described
by James, they are partial in their acceptance of those who
come to worship. To them the cost of a person's clothing is
more important than the attitude of his heart. They are, as
James says, "judges with evil thoughts" (Ja 2:4).

The apostle Paul clearly points out that God often uses
the insignificant things of this earth to accomplish His purposes. We may be impressed by the strong and the mighty,
but God is more interested in that which is sincere and in
those who are true and genuine.

In fact, God places an important estimate on lowliness.
Speaking to the church at Corinth Paul declares that "God
hath chosen the foolish things of the world to confound the
wise; and God hath chosen the weak things of the world to

confound the things which are mighty; and base things of the world, and things which are despised, hath God chosen, yea, and things which are not, to bring to nought things that are." Why? "That no flesh should glory in his presence" (1 Co 1:27-29).

My friend, never forget that! Some people are too smart to care. Others are too high and mighty to be interested in the things of God. To many, God's Word is nothing more than foolishness.

I suppose I have learned some of my greatest lessons from the poor, those whom the world would consider of little importance. What a serious mistake it is to fall into the pitfall of prejudice. God's grace is extended to all men everywhere. Regardless of their position or worth, all men stand equal at the foot of the cross!

D. L. Moody had a tremendous burden for the downtrodden and neglected. Sunday after Sunday he would travel up and down the streets of Chicago, gathering the tattered little children into the Sunday school. On one occasion Moody promised a class of thirteen boys that if they would maintain good conduct and attend Sunday school regularly through the summer and fall, he would give each of them a new suit of clothes for Christmas. Twelve of the boys earned their suits, and Moody had them photographed in their ragged clothes first, captioning it, *Will It Pay?* then in their new suits, labeling that, *It Does Pay!* About 1858, Moody opened his own Sunday school in an old saloon building. It soon became so crowded that the mayor of Chicago offered him the North Market Hall for a meeting place. As founder and director, he filled a variety of offices, from janitor to superintendent.

"Sunday was a busy day for me then," Moody wrote. "During the week I would be out of town selling boots and shoes, but I would always manage to be back by Saturday night.

Often it was late when I got to my room, but I would have to be up by six o'clock to get the hall ready for Sunday school.

"Every Saturday night a German society had a dance there, and I had to roll out the beer kegs, sweep up the sawdust, clean up generally and arrange the chairs. This usually took most of the morning, and then I had to go out to drum up the scholars.

"By the time two o'clock came we would have the hall full, and then I had to keep order while the speaker of the day led the exercises. . . . When school was over I visited absent scholars and found out why they were not at Sunday school, called on the sick, and invited parents to attend the evening gospel service." Moody was no respector of persons. He had a love for all men, rich and poor alike.

To this day a plaque appears at the entrance of Moody Church which reads, "Ever welcome to this house of God are the strangers and the poor."

Another great man of God, John Wesley, concentrated much of his ministry among the poor who were rejected by the regular church. Much of the social legislation which swept England during the eighteenth century, bringing humane treatment to young and old alike, was a result of his concern for the neglected.

Unfortunately many Christians today have become pampered and spoiled by things and possessions. We have become so comfortable and smug that we have practically forgotten about a lost and needy world. May that not be so! The inclusive gospel cannot be shared by an exclusive people. Classism, racism, and all other forms of prejudice are not consistent with the grace of God.

Although the poor were predominant, the early church was made up of all types of people, rich and poor. There was a place for Nicodemus, the Jewish leader, as well as the Samaritan woman. There was room for Onesimus, the slave, as well as for Philemon, his master. There was wealthy Barnabas, who shared his riches with the masses, and there were the poor who had nothing to share. All types of people made up that first church, and yet each one shared a love and concern for all the others.

You know that is the same kind of love that Jesus expressed for each one of us. Paul says, "Ye know the grace of our Lord Jesus Christ, that, though he was rich, yet for your sakes he became poor, that ye through his poverty might be rich" (2 Co 8:9). He who possessed all the wealth and power that heaven afforded, was willing to lay aside His riches and come to the earth and die so that you and I might partake in the riches of eternal life.

I wonder, my friend, is your life characterized by that kind of love for other people? Do you show compassion and concern for all mankind? Or are you a "respector of persons"?

RESPECT OF PERSONS IS INCONSISTENT WITH GOD'S LAW

James tells us that not only is prejudice inconsistent with the grace of God, but it is also contrary to God's law. In chapter 2, verses 8 and 9, James says, "If you fulfil the royal law according to the scripture, Thou shalt love thy neighbour as thyself, you do well: but if you have respect to persons, you commit sin." Yes, prejudice is inconsistent with God's law. To label people as worthy and unworthy, as good and bad, as acceptable and repulsive, is contrary to God's law and thoroughly anti-Christian. In Jesus Christ, "There is neither Jew nor Greek . . . bond nor free . . . male nor female" (Gal 3:28).

What is the royal law? In Leviticus 19:18 we read, "Thou shalt love thy neighbour as thyself: I am the LORD." Jesus endorsed this in Matthew 19:19, "Honour thy father and thy mother: and, Thou shalt love thy neighbour as thyself." Love of God and love of man, who is made in God's image, is God's law.

Respect of persons is not merely an error of judgment or a breach of etiquette—it is a violation of God's royal law. God's Word plainly teaches the equality of all humanity. God is the Creator of all mankind. In His sight all are equal. God has no favorites.

The Bible says that when Jesus "saw the multitudes, he was moved with compassion on them, because they fainted, and were scattered abroad, as sheep having no shepherd" (Mt 9:36). The word *compassion* is actually made up of two words—*con*, meaning "together" or "with," and *passion*, meaning "to suffer." Jesus "suffered with" the multitudes. He was moved by their needs. He did not choose certain ones upon whom to bestow His love. He had "compassion" on all the people.

If we as Christians are going to accomplish anything for Jesus Christ in this generation, we must possess an attitude of unselfish love for *all* mankind.

Respect of persons is sin

Respect of persons is inconsistent with God's grace. It is inconsistent with God's law. In fact, respect of persons is an act of sin. Classism and racism are an insult to God. "But if ye have respect to persons, ye commit sin, and are convinced of the law as transgressors" (Ja 2:9).

A young boy grew up in the streets of New York City. His mother was Puerto Rican, his father was a Negro. He never really knew where he belonged. He trusted no one, and his days and nights were filled with hatred and rebellion. From gang fighting he turned to narcotics. Heroin became his god. And because he had learned the power of fear early, he became a stickup artist. It was routine for him to hold a knife against someone's throat in order to get money for drugs.

Then one day he stumbled into a little church. It was not beautiful to look at, it had cracks in the walls, but the love of Jesus Christ flowed out to soften his tough heart in a way he had never known before. No one there that day commented on his dirty clothes. No one told him to sit in the back row of seats. Instead, the leader offered to give him food and a clean bed.

Through the services which spoke of God's love for him, and through the personal counseling that the pastor gave, the deep wounds in that boy's heart began to heal. The love he now contains makes life not a hateful indignity to escape but an opportunity to help others know the filling of God's Spirit.

My friend, all of us are guilty of showing prejudice to those around us. Perhaps you have been partial in your treatment of other people—men and women for whom Christ died. God's Word tells us that attitudes and actions of prejudice are not just minor mistakes. They are a violation of God's law, open and outright sin against God Himself. Let us humbly repent of our sin, seeking to express our concern and love to all men everywhere.

- "But if ye have respect to persons, ye commit sin, and are convinced of the law as transgressors" (Ja 2:9).
- God is the Creator of the universe! He loves all of His creation, and He is no respector of persons.
- God is color-blind to skin.
- The inclusive gospel cannot be shared by an exclusive people.
- To label people as worthy and unworthy, as good and bad, as acceptable and repulsive, is contrary to God's law and thoroughly anti-Christian.

What doth it profit, my brethren, though a man say he hath faith, and have not works? can faith save him?

If a brother or sister be naked, and destitute of daily food,

And one of you say unto them, Depart in peace, be ye warmed and filled; notwithstanding ye give them not those things which are needful to the body; what doth it profit?

Even so faith, if it hath not works, is dead, being alone.

Yea, a man may say, Thou hast faith, and I have works: shew me thy faith without thy works, and I will shew thee my faith by my works.

Thou believest that there is one God; thou doest well: the devils also believe, and tremble.

But wilt thou know, O vain man, that faith without works is dead?

Was not Abraham our father justified by works, when he had offered Isaac his son upon the altar?

Seest thou how faith wrought with his works, and by works was faith made perfect?

And the scripture was fulfilled which saith, Abraham believed God, and it was imputed unto him for righteousness: and he was called the Friend of God.

Ye see then how that by works a man is justified, and not by faith only.

Likewise also was not Rahab the harlot justified by works, when she had received the messengers, and had sent them out another way?

For as the body without the spirit is dead, so faith without works is dead also.

JAMES 2:14-26

6

Faith That Works

Many people in this world think that God keeps a big scale on which He weighs our behavior here on earth. If the good which we do in this life outweighs the bad, then God will one day welcome us to heaven.

Because of this false idea, millions of people are busy trying to work their way into heaven.

On the other hand, there are many true believers in Christ who look upon good works as something that the Christian should avoid.

What is the answer? Is it "faith" or "works" that determines our eternal destiny?

Faith means many things to many people. To some, like the agnostic Voltaire, faith "consists of believing things only because they are impossible." H. L. Mencken expressed the same sentiment when he mockingly said, "Faith is an illogical belief in the occurrence of the impossible."

But to millions of people faith is not only possible, it is also as John Wesley declared, "the divine evidence whereby the spiritual man discerneth God and the things of God."

The epistle of James is often referred to as "the epistle of faith in action." James's entire letter is devoted to a discussion of how the believer can show his faith. It is really a blueprint for "faith that works."

James 2:14-26 presents us with one of the most controversial portions in this entire epistle. It is because of *this* section that Martin Luther referred to the book of James as "a veritable epistle of straw." Why did Luther say this? Well, Luther, at one point in his life, believed that James' words regarding "works" were a contradiction of the teachings of the apostle Paul.

What is the reason for all this controversy? Does James actually prescribe works as a necessity for salvation? Is eternal life something that has to be earned? In chapter 2 of this epistle, James declares, "What doth it profit, my brethren, though a man say he hath faith, and have not works? Can faith save him" (2:14)? "Even so faith, if it hath not works, is dead, being alone. Yea, a man may say, Thou hast faith, and I have works: show me thy faith without thy works, and I will show thee my faith by my works" (2:17-18).

If we compare these words with Paul's writing in the book of Romans, we discover some of the cause of Luther's criticism. Because in Romans 3:28 we read, "Therefore we conclude that a man is justified *by faith* without the deeds of the law." To the German reformer, the words of James appeared to be a contradiction to Paul. He looked upon this epistle as a defense of the legalism which he had earlier experienced in the Medieval church.

Martin Luther had for years been an Augustinian monk. Prior to the Reformation he had spent his entire life in the church. From his youth he had been indoctrinated with the teachings of indulgence, penance, and good deeds.

Then through his reading of Paul's epistles to the Romans and Galatians, Luther understood that salvation does not come through good works or deeds of the body—but by faith in the finished work of Jesus Christ alone. It was this discovery that led to his salvation experience.

"When," said Luther, "by the Spirit of God I understood these words, 'The just shall live by faith,' I felt born again like a new man; I entered through the open doors into the very paradise of God!"

Before his conversion Luther's life had largely consisted of rules, works, and tradition. Like Paul, he turned from this life, and declared salvation to be by faith alone! Undoubtedly Luther's criticism of James was influenced by his background. But the question remains—is there really a conflict between the writings of James and Paul? Did these two leaders preach different doctrines?

In my estimation the answer is no! Although Paul's teaching may outwardly appear to contradict James, there are several things that must be considered.

First, when Paul uses the word *works* he is referring to a legalistic observance of the Jewish law. Many Jewish converts in the early church were still "working" at the tradition and ritual of Judaism. Paul stresses that salvation is a gift and not a result of legalistic works.

On the other hand, *James* uses the word *works* to refer to fruit. The fruit of real salvation is obedience. Jesus Himself proclaimed that, "By their fruits ye shall know them" (Mt 7:20). Works or fruits are the outward example, the proof of a true inward experience.

James says that faith by itself is dead. It is nothing more than an intellectual assent to the fact of God. He condemns an idle faith as being nothing but barren orthodoxy.

Do you have real faith? asks James. Then show it! Give some tangible proof of that which you profess.

Someone has said that true, genuine faith involves verification by the heart, confession by the tongue, and action by the limbs. This is the theme of James' epistle.

On the other hand one of Paul's purposes in writing to the churches at Rome and Galatia was to stop the Jewish Christians from subjecting Gentile believers to Jewish rituals and law. To the church at Ephesus Paul wrote, "By grace are ye saved through faith; and that not of yourselves: it is the gift of God: not of works, lest any man should boast" (Eph 2:8-9). The supposed conflict or contradiction between James and Paul was really a difference of perspective and background. Each man emphasizes a different point, but they both come to the same conclusions.

James preached faith demonstrated by works. His aim was to wake up the self-complacent people who claimed to believe but did little about it. The combination of faith and works as seen in this epistle can be illustrated by the positive and negative particles that are found in an atom. Both are absolutely indispensable for electricity.

An atom contains both negative electron particles and positive proton particles. In a normal atom the charges of the electrons and protons balance, so that when an electron leaves an atom, the atom becomes positively charged. If an electron is added, the atom becomes negatively charged. The electrons cannot say to the protons, "You are not needed," nor can the protons say the same to the electrons.

Faith and works in the life of the Christian unite in much the same way. And although the Scripture clearly indicates that we cannot work our way to heaven, both a vital faith and expression of that faith are extremely important. James says it is ridiculous to say you have faith and then turn your back on every opportunity to demonstrate that faith. If that is how you act, then your faith is not real. It is not genuine. It is false!

A MAKE-BELIEVE FAITH

Verses 15 and 16 of chapter 2 present an example of a make-believe faith. James writes "If a brother or sister be naked, and destitute of daily food, and one of you say unto them, Depart in peace, be ye warmed and filled; notwithstanding ye give them not those things which are needful to the body; what doth it profit?"

These people whom James mentions are not professional beggars. They are brothers and sisters who are in a particular time of deep need. How do we react when this type of need confronts us? Do we say, "God bless you my brother, we'll pray for you. Go in peace and be comfortable"? That is not how Jesus reacted when He saw those in need. The Scriptures tell us that when He saw the multitudes, "he was moved with compassion" (Mt 9:36). He healed the sick, He gave sight to the blind, He gave food to the hungry. He was concerned with the needs all around Him.

James says that if we say we are concerned but do nothing to help our neighbor, our faith is nothing but cheap words. He says, "Faith, if it hath not works, is dead, being alone" (Ja 2:17). It is one thing to talk about faith, but it is something else entirely to demonstrate it. A man may profess to be an expert swimmer, but if he never goes near the water, his claim means very little. James is simply saying that if you say that you have faith, prove it. To use the vernacular of today, "Put your money where your mouth is."

The Bible tells us that on one occasion a rich, young man came to Jesus and asked Him what he must do in order to gain eternal life. He was a good man and very religious. He had kept all the commandments from his youth. But when Jesus responded by telling him that he should sell all his possessions and give the money to the poor—his countenance fell. His faith was really nothing more than make-believe.

Every once in a while someone will come to me and complain about the condition of our youth today. Now I know that some have deep problems, but many of our young people are earnestly seeking for the answers to life. Here at the

Moody Bible Institute we have some of the finest young men and women in the world.

But as I talk to young people from time to time I find that one of their biggest criticisms of the church is the false faith they see all around them—friends, teachers, sometimes even parents who profess one thing but live another.

Oftentimes an individual suffering from schizophrenia will experience hallucinations. He will become withdrawn into his own little make-believe world and pretend that he is something or someone he is not. To the individual it is all very real, but to others it is obvious that the poor man is suffering from some mental disorder.

Too many Christians today seem to suffer from spiritual schizophrenia. They profess to have faith, but in reality their faith is only make-believe.

May God deliver us from a ho-hum attitude. Young people can read their parents. They can see right through their teachers, and they turn away in disgust from a make-believe faith.

An intellectual faith

James not only preaches against a make-believe faith, he also condemns that which is merely an intellectual faith.

It's very easy to sing or say "I believe." That's head faith. But true heart faith—saving faith—produces fruit. Faith without fruit is false!

To simply say "I believe," is of no special merit or value. James tells us that even the demons "believe" in God. According to chapter 2, verse 19 there are no atheists among the demons. They know too much to succumb to unbelief. They have all the head knowledge of God but no heart trust. Theirs is merely a mental assent.

Intellectual faith, my friend, is of no greater value than is make-believe faith. Each one is lacking the "fruit" which must be demonstrated in the life of a true Christian.

An obedient faith

Obedient faith, says James, is the only faith that works. Do you have that kind of faith?

In the last few verses of this chapter we are told about Abraham who was asked by God to do a very difficult thing— to offer his son Isaac upon an altar of sacrifice. The Bible tells us that Abraham believed God. He did not understand why God was asking him to do this, but he believed God. He obeyed God's command, and, just as he was about to offer his son's life, God provided a ram to take Isaac's place on the altar.

In verse 22 James says, "Seest thou how faith wrought with his works, and by works was faith made perfect?" Abraham trusted God so completely that he was willing to obey Him in even the most trying of circumstances. His faith operating in him is that which led him to obey God. As Moffatt suggests, "faith cooperated with deeds." Abraham's obedient faith and resulting works fitted together like hand and glove. His faith was "made perfect"; it was made complete by his works.

Abraham obeyed God completely. His faith was alive. His faith was fruitful. Yes, and *obedient* faith is saving faith. Paul said, "Whosoever shall call upon the name of the Lord shall be saved" (Ro 10:13).

Today some people are afraid of that word, *saved*. Actually it is a great word used numerous times throughout the New Testament. In Acts 4:12 we read, "Neither is there salvation in any other: for there is none other name under heaven given among men, whereby we must be saved."

In Acts 16 the Philippian jailer asked of Paul, "What must

I do to be saved?" Paul replied, "Believe on the Lord Jesus Christ, and thou shalt be saved, and thy house" (Ac 16:30-31).

There are two ingredients in saving faith—repenting and believing. To repent is more than just being sorry for your sins. It involves a change of direction. D. L. Moody used to say, "Man is born with his back toward God. When he repents of his sin, he turns around and starts walking to meet God." Saving faith is not possible unless a man also repents of his sin. True belief, genuine faith, does not come unless we are willing to make a personal surrender of our whole life to Christ.

Once when the great tightrope walker, Blondin, was performing on a cable across Niagara Falls, he asked his audience, "How many of you believe I can walk across that wire pushing a wheelbarrow?" The people all cheered and he then asked, "How many think I can do it with a man in the wheelbarrow?" As his audience cheered again, Blondin pointed to one enthusiastic gentleman and said, "You're my man." Needless to say the man made a rapid escape. He believed all about Blondin's ability, but he was not ready personally to commit himself.

Millions of people in our world today believe *about* Jesus Christ. Some have a make-believe faith. Others hope they can work their way into God's favor. There are some people who have an intellectual faith. They believe Jesus lived and that He was a great teacher, but that is as far as they are willing to go.

The Word of God tells us that true faith is not a vague, mystical thing. It is not merely a mental attitude. It involves a personal and total commitment of oneself to Jesus Christ as Saviour and Lord.

If you, my friend, have never experienced this kind of faith, why not make this the day you totally yield yourself to

Jesus Christ. Put your life into His hands, repent of your sin, and He will give you a faith that works.

- "For as the body without the spirit is dead, so faith without works is dead also" (Ja 2:26).
- James says that faith by itself is dead. It is nothing more than an intellectual assent to the fact of God.
- It's very easy to sing or say "I believe." That's head faith. But true heart faith—saving faith—produces fruit. Faith without fruit is false!
- Obedient faith, says James, is the only faith that works.
- May God deliver us from a ho-hum attitude. Young people can read their parents. They can see right through their teachers, and they turn away in disgust from a make-believe faith.

My brethren, be not many masters, knowing that we shall receive the greater condemnation.

For in many things we offend all. If any man offend not in word, the same is a perfect man, and able also to bridle the whole body.

Behold, we put bits in the horses' mouths, that they may obey us; and we turn about their whole body.

Behold also the ships, which though they be so great, and are driven of fierce winds, yet are they turned about with a very small helm, withersoever the governor listeth.

Even so the tongue is a little member, and boasteth great things. Behold, how great a matter a little fire kindleth!

And the tongue is a fire, a world of iniquity: so is the tongue among our members, that it defileth the whole body, and setteth on fire the course of nature; and it is set on fire of hell.

For every kind of beasts, and of birds, and of serpents, and of things in the sea, is tamed, and hath been tamed of mankind:

But the tongue can no man tame; it is an unruly evil, full of deadly poison.

Therewith bless we God, even the Father; and therewith curse we men, which are made after the similitude of God.

Out of the same mouth proceedeth blessing and cursing. My brethren, these things ought not so to be.

Doth a fountain send forth at the same place sweet water and bitter?

Can the fig tree, my brethren, bear olive berries? either a vine, figs? so can no fountain both yield salt water and fresh.

JAMES 3:1-12

7

Expensive Talk

We are a nation of talkers!

Each week nearly forty-five hours of talk programs are carried over the major television networks. Countless hours of radio time are devoted to talk shows in cities around the country. People everywhere have something to say and want to be heard!

But contrary to popular opinion, talk is not cheap! Indeed, talk can be very expensive.

Recently Dr. Wernher von Braun, the American space pioneer, made some startling predictions concerning mass communications. In an article appearing in the *Astronautics and Aeronautics Journal,* the NASA chief suggested that soon it will be possible to carry out so many different kinds of transactions within the home, that people will be able to live anywhere. Home communication centers will make office buildings, banks, and stores almost obsolete. Direct visual and audio communication will be possible with anyone at anytime and anywhere.

In contrast to the old-fashioned coaxial cable that could handle only one television channel at a time and a few hundred telephone calls, von Braun foresees nuclear lasers handling thousands of television channels along with *billions* of telephone conversations all at the same time.

Unfortunately, with all our advancement in technology, many people today are speaking, but very few people are listening.

In his 1969 inaugural address, President Richard Nixon told the nation, "America has suffered from a fever of words. We cannot learn from one another until we stop shouting at one another—until we speak quietly enough so that our words can be heard as well as our voices."

The apostle James, writing to Christians, said, "Let every man be swift to hear, slow to speak, slow to wrath" (Ja 1:19).

After already drawing our attention to the control of the tongue in chapter 1, James returns to this vital subject in chapter 3. In fact, the matter of self-discipline in our speech is of such importance that James devotes twelve verses to the subject of our tongues in this important chapter.

The tongue is an amazing instrument. Although it is of relatively small size, it is an extremely important member of the body. Often the tongue is a guidepost to our physical well-being. By examining the tongue a doctor can determine much relating to our health. In many respects this same member of our body can also reveal much concerning our spiritual condition.

James obviously was aware of the tongue problems which existed among the believers at Jerusalem as well as elsewhere. As Plummer suggests, James is here speaking directly to those who, "substitute words for works." In chapter 3 verse 1, he warns against being quick to criticize and condemn. It is so easy for our speech to get out of control.

The tongue is the instrument given to us by God to enable us to express how we think and feel. It in turn can become our strongest asset or our greatest liability. The tongue can be a beautiful angel or a hideous demon. It can be pure or vile. It can caress or cut. The tongue can arouse men to act as well as it can subdue their emotions. A false whisper can infuriate a nation, but the power of eloquence can quell the fury of a multitude. A word of anger can wound, while a word of kindness can win. Words of hate can kill and words of love can comfort. God says: "Death and life are in the power of the tongue" (Pro 18:21).

THE POWER OF THE TONGUE

Yes, my friend, the tongue is powerful!

The eloquence of Bernard of Clairvaux was so great that thousands of people felt compelled to leave their earthly goods behind them and join Europe's Second Crusade.

The rousing delivery of Patrick Henry's immortal words, "Give me liberty or give me death!" inspired the struggling colonies to fight on and secure their national liberty.

Who today will ever forget the stirring words of the young president, John Kennedy, "Ask not what your country can do for you—ask what you can do for your country."

The tongue is powerful!

Princes and peasants, countries and continents, towns and cities have been pushed by careless words into bloody battle. Because of angry words, brothers have fought until one dripped with the other's blood; children have forsaken their homes; and best of friends have become bitter enemies. Husbands and wives have been separated forever by a cutting tongue.

James knew well the power of the tongue. He compared it to two devices—the bit which controls a horse, and the rudder which guides a ship. "Behold, we put bits in the horses' mouths, that they may obey us; and we turn about their whole body" (Ja 3:3).

The horse is a large, strong animal. Many years ago he roamed wild. Yet the bit, part of a bridle, has brought the horse into subjection. The human tongue also will yield to a firm, kind touch of the reins.

Peter said, "He that will love life, and see good days, let him refrain his tongue from evil, and his lips that they speak no guile" (1 Pe 3:10).

One slogan used during World War II was, "a slip of the lip may sink a ship." I have a picture of a South Pacific battle scene in which Marines are storming a beachhead. They are dropping everywhere. One Marine is wounded and bleeding. The picture bears a two-word title: *Somebody Talked*. It may be that the tongue has slain more than have all the bullets and bombs of battle. The book of Proverbs tells us that "A soft tongue breaketh the bone" (Pro 25:15*b*). And again we read, "He that keepeth his mouth keepeth his life" (Pro 13:3).

James also compares the tongue to a ship's rudder. "Behold also the ships, which though they be so great, and are driven of fierce winds, yet are they turned about with a very small helm, whithersoever the governor listeth" (Ja 3:4).

The rudder is not large in size, yet its decisive motion is that which turns the entire ship. The pilot turns the helm, and the vessel changes its course. So the course of a life can be changed by the utterance of a few words.

Twenty-five years ago, I stood in front of a minister with my beautiful bride. When he asked if I would take this young lady to be my wife, I enthusiastically said, "I will." Those two words happily changed the course of my life.

A prisoner stood before a judge. The judge turned and said, "Guilty." One word changed the course of the accused man's life.

What the rudder is to the ship, the tongue is to the body. James is saying that to avoid shipwreck—control your tongue!

THE PERILS OF THE TONGUE

Not only is the tongue a mighty power, but it is also a dangerous peril!

"Even so," said James, "the tongue is a little member, and boasteth great things. Behold, how great a matter a little fire kindleth! And the tongue is a fire, a world of iniquity: so is the tongue among our members, that it defileth the whole body" (Ja 3:5-6). Moffatt translates this, "What a forest is set ablaze by a little spark of fire."

We hear much today, and rightly so, concerning the devastation that occurs each year in our national forests because of careless campers and thoughtless smokers. One match can destroy a forest that has taken a hundred years to grow.

Fire spreads quickly and is soon out of control. One can gossip and then ask God to forgive him. God will forgive, but He alone knows where that gossip will stop. It goes on and on, burning and destroying.

Morgan Blake, sportswriter for the *Atlanta Journal*, wrote:

> I am more deadly than the screaming shell from the howitzer. I win without killing. I tear down homes, break hearts, and wreck lives. I travel on the wings of the wind. No innocence is strong enough to intimidate me, no purity pure enough to daunt me. I have no regard for truth, no respect for justice, no mercy for the defenseless. My victims are as numerous as the sands of the sea, and often as innocent. I never forget and seldom forgive. My name is Gossip.

We can never stop the consequences of a lie. We may explain it, or we may prove it false; yet sooner or later someone will revive the hideous tale.

A fiery tongue is like a burning match in a gasoline tank. The tongue ignites a great fire. A word of hate inflames opposition. A mocking word incites bitterness. An evil word may kindle a career of sin. A foul word heard on the streets, in the shop, or in the school, may start fires burning within until nothing is left but ashes.

Contentious tongues have hindered the work of God a thousand times over. Critical tongues have closed church doors. Careless tongues have broken the hearts and health of many pastors. The sins of the tongue have besmirched the pure white garments of the bride of Christ. "The tongue is a fire . . . and it is set on fire of hell" (Ja 3:6).

But there is also a heavenly fire. There is a clean fire. Acts 2 refers to "cloven tongues like as of fire" (Ac 2:3). Isaiah 6 speaks of the purifying fire of God which touched and cleansed the lips of the prophet.

Which fire have you experienced? Clean or unclean—the fire which comes from heaven or that which originates in hell?

God's Word also tells us that the tongue is untameable. "For every kind of beasts, and of birds, and of serpents, and of things in the sea, is tamed, and hath been tamed by mankind: but the tongue can no man tame" (Ja 3:7-8). In the beginning God gave man dominion over every animal (Gen 1:28). We can tame the horse of the field. We can tame the birds of the air. Even fish have been tamed! But no man can tame the tongue.

In this age of unparalleled technology we have seen man's creative ability result in the taming of nearly all the earth's elements. We have conquered the land, the sea, and even outer space. But we cannot conquer the tongue.

The tongue is sometimes like a whip whose impact produces ugly scars which no doctor can heal. It is like a razor-sharp sword which cuts deep, mortal wounds. The tongue is sometimes a beast trampling ignorantly over precious diamonds.

No man can tame the tongue. But I have good news for you—no man can, but Jesus can.

There once was a madman in the land of Gadara. At midnight, he would scream and cause the whole countryside to tremble. Often the calm of the evening was torn by his cry. The Bible tells us that "no man could tame him."

One day this man met Jesus and cried, "What have I to do with thee, Jesus, thou Son of the most high God?" Jesus said, "Come out of the man, thou unclean spirit" (Mk 5:7-8), and the demons came out. The untameable had been tamed.

"And he went his way," the Scriptures tell us, "and published throughout the whole city how great things Jesus had done unto him" (Lk 8:39). No man could tame his tongue, but Jesus did.

Saul of Tarsus had a wicked tongue that scoffed at the early Christians, but Jesus tamed it and made it eloquent in praise.

What about you? Perhaps you have a careless tongue. Let Jesus tame it. Perhaps you have a censoring tongue. Let Jesus tame it. No man can tame the tongue, but Jesus can. The secret of a governable tongue is not self-control but Christ-control. The Lord Jesus had an impressive tongue. The prophet declared, "neither was any deceit in his mouth" (Isa 53:9).

James continues by telling us the tongue "is an unruly evil, full of deadly poison" (Ja 3:8b). The words of the tongue can be more deadly than the poison of a snake. Paul says, "The poison of asps is under their lips" (Ro 3:13b). Solomon proclaimed, "A fool's mouth is his destruction, and his lips are the snare of his soul. The words of a talebearer are as wounds, and they go down into the innermost parts of the belly" (Pro 18:7-8).

The love of Christ is the only antidote to the poison of the tongue. Paul tells the Ephesian Christians to "let no corrupt communication proceed out of your mouth, but that which is good to the use of edifying, that it may minister grace unto the hearers" (Eph 4:29).

THE PERVERSITY OF THE TONGUE

There are two ways in which we can use the tongue. Either we use it to bless or we use it to curse. All which honors God is blessing. And all that dishonors man, who is in God's image, may be called cursing.

James asks: "Doth a fountain send forth at the same place sweet water and bitter? Can the fig tree, my brethren, bear olive berries? Either a vine, figs? So can no fountain both yield salt water and fresh" (Ja 3:11-12).

Nature has no confusion in her plans. A fountain sends forth sweet water or bitter. A fig tree bears figs; the vine bears grapes. But man, the highest of God's creatures, is confused. He blesses with one breath and curses with the next. If we bless God when we look up to Him and curse Him when we see His likeness in our fellow men, then our cursing is prevailing.

Someone has suggested, "To blow a spark will cause it to burn. To spit on it will put it out. Both are from the mouth." Let us never start fire with our words; let us never add to them, but put them out.

Edward Everett Hale in his story *The Man Without a Country* tells of the young naval officer, Philip Nolan, who with some others was on trial for being false to the service.

As the court session dragged on and the trial came to a close, Nolan was asked if he wished to say anything to show that he had always been faithful to the United States. In a fit of temper he cursed and said, "I wish that I may never hear of the United States again!"

The judge and the jury were shocked! In fifteen minutes they issued the verdict: "The Court decides, subject to the approval of the President, that you shall never hear the name of the United States again." Nolan laughed, but no one else laughed, and he became the man without a country.

We have all been guilty, not of fifteen idle words, but of fifteen million idle words. And we must beg God's forgiveness! "If we confess our sins," says John, "[God] is faithful and just to forgive us our sins, and to cleanse us from all unrighteousness" (1 Jn 1:9). The word *confess* is made of two Greek words which mean "to speak or say the same thing." You and I must come to the place where we will say about our sin exactly what God has already said.

A young man had cancer of the tongue. Before the operation the doctor told him that he would never speak again. The young man paused and then said, "Thank God for Jesus Christ." What beautiful last words.

Paul writes, "God also hath highly exalted him . . . that at the name of Jesus every knee should bow . . . and that every tongue should confess that Jesus Christ is Lord, to the glory of God the Father" (Phil 2:9-11).

My friend, will you confess Jesus Christ as Saviour right now? It is not a question of whether you will confess Christ— but of when—God says every tongue shall confess. You will! Will you do it later, compelled by judgment, or will you, of your own volition, do it now?

Say with Frances Havergal,

> "Take my lips, and let them be
> Filled with messages for Thee."

Pray with David, "Let the words of my mouth, and the meditation of my heart, be acceptable in thy sight, O LORD, my strength, and my redeemer" (Ps 19:14).

- "But the tongue can no man tame; it is an unruly evil, full of deadly poison" (Ja 3:8).
- What the rudder is to the ship, the tongue is to the body. James is saying, "To avoid shipwreck—control your tongue.
- No man can tame the tongue. But I have good news for you—no man can, but Jesus can.
- The secret of a governable tongue is not self-control but Christ-control.

Who is a wise man and endued with knowledge among you? let him shew out of a good conversation his works with meekness of wisdom.

But if ye have bitter envying and strife in your hearts, glory not, and lie not against the truth.

This wisdom descendeth not from above, but is earthly, sensual, devilish.

For where envying and strife is, there is confusion and every evil work.

But the wisdom that is from above is first pure, then peaceable, gentle, and easy to be intreated, full of mercy and good fruits, without partiality, and without hypocrisy.

And the fruit of righteousness is sown in peace of them that make peace.

JAMES 3:13-18

8

Wisdom from Above

Someone has said that learning is like rowing a boat upstream; if you don't go forward you are really going backwards. We all agree that knowledge is important. In fact, most of us learn something new every day.

But have you ever considered the fact that knowledge in itself is not enough? The Bible tells us that divine wisdom is the key to happiness and a successful life. Solomon said, "Wisdom is the principal thing; therefore get wisdom" (Pro 4:7).

Recent statistics show that in 1972, in the United States alone, more than forty-five million children were enrolled in our public schools, over six million young people attended our colleges and universities, and tens of thousands more participated in special job training programs.

Never before in our nation's history has there been such a knowledge explosion! Never before has there been so much opportunity for learning, literally from the cradle to the grave. Today, formal education begins as the two-year-old sits in front of the television set and is taught the fundamentals of reading. Any man, woman, or child today can receive an education. Illiteracy is practically a thing of the past.

And yet as we witness this tremendous learning epidemic,

it is revealing to notice that education in itself has not proved to be the answer to our basic problems. Unfortunately, with all our knowledge, we have accumulated very little wisdom.

As we study the Bible, we find that wisdom is the key to success—both with God *and* with man. Solomon wrote, "Wisdom is better than rubies; and all the things that may be desired are not to be compared to it" (Pro 8:11).

THE NEED FOR WISDOM

What is wisdom? The dictionary describes it as the "understanding of what is true, right, and lasting." In other words, the wise man is the man who is able to make the right choices. He has a proper sense of values, he knows what things in life really matter, and his decisions and actions are determined accordingly. Our wisdom is not determined by how much knowledge we possess. A man may be highly educated and yet never know true wisdom. On the other hand, there are many who know the true meaning of wisdom, but who have never received a formal education.

In James 3:13 the writer asks the question, "Who is a wise man and endued with knowledge among you? Let him show out of a good [life] his works with meekness of wisdom." James' question does not imply that no one is wise. The writer here is simply saying that, if your profess to be wise, then make sure your way of living backs it up.

Obviously James is writing here with a particular audience in mind. In the preceding passage he had addressed himself to those who were not genuine in their faith and love for Jesus Christ. Those who were uncontrolled in their speech were the very ones responsible for the dissemination of false teaching. Here James gets to the root of the problem by pointing out that these "wise men" were really not so wise after all. Their false, or fake, wisdom was actually that which was responsible for the creation of controversy in the church.

False teaching was not uncommon in the first century church. The numerous sects and philosophical groups of that day were a continual problem for the early believers. Several epistles in the New Testament were written with the primary purpose of combatting the heresies these groups espoused. In many respects the situation James describes was much like our present religious climate—theological creeds were a dime a dozen.

Throughout this letter James attacks the phony. Time and again he hammers out the need for true and genuine faith—faith that works, that is alive!

In James' day, even as today, there were many fakes, many charlatans and deceivers. Acts chapter 8 tells of one of these, Simon Magus, a false leader of Samaria who pretended to possess supernatural powers. Despite his trickery, many of that day believed him and followed after him.

When Simon saw the power of the Holy Spirit working through the apostles, he offered money that he might purchase their powers. He said, "Give me also this power, that on whomsoever I lay hands, he may receive the Holy Ghost. But Peter said unto him, Thy money perish with thee, because thou hast thought that the gift of God may be purchased with money" (Ac 8:19-20).

Peter really said, Both you and your money will go to hell because you are a fake! "Thou hast neither part nor lot in this matter: for thy heart is not right in the sight of God" (Ac 8:21).

God hates hypocrisy! There are no words strong enough to convey His feelings toward the phony. James is saying, Make sure your actions match your words. It's better to live right than to talk right. The greatest asset you have is your life—a life above accusation!

James says the wise man should "show out of a good *life* his *works*"—not just the externals or stage effects, not just an outward show. The wise is to show forth a transformed life, a life transformed by Jesus Christ.

Many people never read the gospel in a fine leather cover. Some even seem to avoid the inexpensive Bible portions that are distributed by the millions. But no one can escape from the gospel in shoe leather.

The wise man, the man who has been given wisdom from above, is the man whose life is an open book testifying to the saving grace of Jesus Christ.

EARTHLY WISDOM AND ITS CHARACTERISTICS

In this same portion of Scripture, James describes *earthly* wisdom—the wisdom of this world. "But if ye have bitter envying and strife in your hearts, glory not, and lie not against the truth. This wisdom descendeth not from above, but is earthly, sensual, devilish. For where envying and strife is, there is confusion and every evil work" (Ja 3:14-16).

Earthly wisdom is characterized by bitter envying and strife. What is envy? It is our discontent at the good fortune of others.

It was envy that led Cain to become the world's first murderer. God had shown His pleasure and acceptance of Abel's sacrifice, and Cain became envious and slew his brother.

It was because of envy that Joseph was sold by his brothers to be a slave in Egypt.

It was envy that gripped King Saul's heart as he heard the fair maidens singing the praises of David.

Envy is a characteristic of human earthly wisdom. It is earthly and not from above. It exists not only among relatives, but is general toward the well-favored. It is a disease that not only disturbs the mind, but consumes the body as well. In Proverbs 14:30 we read, "A sound heart is the life of the flesh: but envy the rottenness of the bones."

I know a Christian housewife who is outwardly very charming, talented, and intelligent, and yet she is totally frustrated. She is so envious of her sister she is near mental collapse.

Envy eats at the mind like a moth eats at a garment. It is like a cancer as it grows in intensity.

The great G. Campbell Morgan was pastor of Westminster Chapel in London at the same time F. B. Meyer was pastor of nearby Christ's Church and Charles H. Spurgeon was pastor of the Metropolitan Chapel. Both Morgan and Spurgeon often had much larger audiences than did Meyer. Troubled by envy, Meyer confessed that not until he began praying for his colleagues did he have peace of heart. "When I prayed for their success," said Meyer, "the result was that God filled their churches so full that the overflow filled mine, and it has been full since."

Envy is a characteristic of human wisdom. It weights us down, and it leads to sorrow and frustration.

Another sign of earthly wisdom is strife. We are living in an age of strife! Quarreling in the home, discord in the office, antagonism in school—all are facts of life for most people.

We have been bombarded with so much violence on our television screens, in our magazines and newspapers, that we have become as some psychologists suggest, "a violent generation."

And yet God's Word tells us that violence and strife are of the flesh—they are the result of human wisdom, and they have no place in the life of the Christian.

Where do these things come from? James says these characteristics are the result of wisdom that is "not from above, but that which is earthly, sensual, devilish" (Ja 3:15). This, my friend, is human wisdom, and it results in "confusion and every evil work."

HEAVENLY WISDOM AND ITS CHARACTERISTICS

Genesis 1:2 pictures a time when the world was in a chaotic state. The Scripture reads, "The earth was without form, and void; and darkness was upon the face of the deep." Confusion reigned. But then God spoke. He said, "Let there be light." He dispelled the darkness and confusion. He established order, and "he saw . . . that it was good" (Gen 1:4). Heavenly wisdom is the answer to earth's conflicts.

Today, my friend, God wants to say, "Let there be light." He wants to solve your problems and to rearrange your life. If you will let Him, Jesus Christ will give you purpose, direction, and satisfaction.

God will give you His divine, heavenly wisdom if you will but ask of Him. Back in the first chapter of his epistle, James says, "If any . . . lack wisdom, let him ask of God, that giveth to all men liberally" (Ja 1:5).

God's wisdom knows nothing of envy and strife. It is not characterized by disorder and confusion. His wisdom is as different from human wisdom as day is from night, as light is from darkness. In James 3:17 we read that "the wisdom that is from above [God's wisdom] is first pure, then peaceable, gentle, and easy to be intreated, full of mercy and good fruits, without partiality, and without hypocrisy."

James says that God's wisdom is *first* pure! Heavenly wisdom rejects immorality, lying, and cheating. An impure person cannot be wise! He may be very clever—but he will be foolish and unwise in God's sight. Purity is paramount in gaining wisdom.

Paul instructed Timothy, his young son in the faith, to keep himself pure (1 Ti 5:22). Jesus said, "Blessed are the pure in heart: for they shall see God" (Mt 5:8). God's wisdom is first of all pure.

Heavenly wisdom is also peaceable. Romans 12:18 says, "If it be possible, as much as lieth in you, live peaceably with

all men." The man who possesses God's wisdom will be a
seeker of peace. Yes, we must "contend for the faith," we
must struggle in opposition to evil, but "if it be possible" we
are to live peaceably. "Blessed are the peacemakers: for they
shall be called the children of God" (Mt 5:9).

James also tells us that "the wisdom that is from above is
. . . gentle" (Ja 3:17). The word *gentle* indicates "a sweet
reasonableness." Oftentimes it is possible for us to win an
argument but in the process to lose the person with whom we
argue. We must be strong and firm in our convictions and
in our service for Christ, but we must be gentle with those to
whom we minister. Paul wrote in 2 Corinthians 10:1, "I . . .
beseech you by the *meekness* and *gentleness* of Christ" (italics added). How gentle our Lord was! Human wisdom produces strife, but God's wisdom is gentle.

Heavenly wisdom is easy to intreat. It is approachable.
It is characterized by an open mindedness, a willingness to
share—to consider others.

I have known some people who have held grudges for
years. Some churches are divided right down the middle by
warring factions and grudge-holding members. Some folks
never forgive one who has erred. James says that divine wisdom is not obstinate but easy to be intreated.

God's wisdom is also "full of mercy and good fruits." God's
wisdom produces more than leaves—it produces fruit-bearing
Christians. Mercy is the active principle of divine love. This
heavenly wisdom bears good wholesome fruit. The plural,
"fruits," shows that there is abundance for all.

I think of Stephen, "full of faith and of the Holy Ghost"
who, Luke says, "did great wonders and miracles among the
people" (Ac 6:5, 8). I think of Dorcas, a woman of Joppa
who was "full of good works" (Ac 9:36). I am reminded of
John's description of Jesus, "the only begotten of the Father,
full of grace and truth" (Jn 1:14).

My friend, we are to be "full of mercy and good fruits." We are to show love and kindness toward those in need. A truly wise man is a tender man—and one who reproduces his faith in the lives of others.

Finally, James tells us that wisdom that is from above is "without partiality and without hypocrisy." This word occurs nowhere else in the New Testament. It is rendered "without wrangling," "without judging," "without distinction." With the truly wise man there is no first, second, or third class. There are no rich and poor, no black and white. All men stand as equals at the foot of the cross. And although some may fear to preach the whole gospel, afraid that they may offend certain people, our message at the Moody Bible Institute is the whole gospel. Our invitation and concern is for all lost people.

My friend, are these characteristics of your life? Is your life controlled by God's wisdom—that which is from above? Or are you troubled by envy and strife and the confusion that comes when you try to run things your own way?

How to experience heavenly wisdom

This wisdom can be yours by a simple, yet deliberate, act of faith. Some time ago a woman told me how that all of her life she had longed for peace and the qualities of heavenly wisdom. Following high school she had married—but that did not make her happy. She had no real communication with her husband beyond the physical level. She had one baby after another, and soon she was living just for her four children. Life was an empty routine of strife and confusion.

One day she was invited by a friend to one of our meetings, and she soon realized that in the gospel of Jesus Christ her needs could be met. Upon accepting Jesus Christ as her personal Saviour she literally came alive.

Despite the great joy that she had realized, she was aware

that there was still a great gulf between her husband and the Lord. In counseling with her I pointed out that she was the key to winning her family for Christ. She began to substitute heavenly wisdom for her own human wisdom, and immediately things began to happen.

The Holy Spirit taught her how to avoid strife. Her housekeeping improved. She became gentle and easy to entreat. She even worked off some excess pounds and became more concerned about her personal appearance.

A short time later she came back to see me and said, "You know, Dr. Sweeting, the other day my husband kissed me and said, 'Things have certainly been different, Darling!'" Then she said, "You know, it's really working."

Yes, my friend, God's wisdom does work, and it will work for you if you will let Jesus Christ have absolute control.

In the third century, Cyprian, the Bishop of Carthage, wrote to his friend Donatus: "It is a bad world, Donatus, an incredibly bad world. But I have discovered in the midst of it a quiet and good people who have learned the great secret of life. They have found a joy and wisdom which is a thousand times better than any of the pleasures of our sinful life. They are despised and persecuted, but they care not. They are masters of their souls. They have overcome the world. These people, Donatus, are Christians . . . and I am one of them."

If you have repented of your sins and have received Christ as Saviour, then you, too, are one of them.

Ask God in faith for heavenly wisdom because this is God's way to solve conflicts.

■ "But the wisdom that is from above is first pure, then peaceable, gentle, and easy to be intreated, full of mercy and good fruits, without partiality, and without hypocrisy" (Ja 3:17).

- The greatest asset you have is your life—a life above accusation!

- James says that God's wisdom is *first* pure! Heavenly wisdom rejects immorality, lying, and cheating. An impure person cannot be wise! He may be very clever—but he will be foolish and unwise in God's sight. Purity is paramount in gaining wisdom.

- Many people never read the gospel in a fine leather cover. . . . But no one can escape from the gospel in shoe leather.

*From whence come wars and fightings among you?
come they not hence, even of your lusts that war in your
members?*

*Ye lust, and have not: ye kill, and desire to have, and
cannot obtain: ye fight and war, yet ye have not, because
ye ask not.*

*Ye ask, and receive not, because ye ask amiss, that ye
may consume it upon your lusts.*

JAMES 4:1-3

9

Why Do We Have Conflict?

Not long ago a Norwegian statistician computerized every war that had ever been fought. His study quickly indicated that during 5,560 years of recorded history there have been 14,531 wars, averaging a little over 2.6 wars each year. In the history of 185 generations, only 10 of those generations have witnessed unbroken peace.

It is quite obvious that, throughout the ages, war has been the rule on earth, and peace has been the exception.

Why is this so? What is the cause of our conflicts? Why do we have war?

These questions have been asked by men throughout the ages. And for every asking there has been a suggested answer. Nicholas Rowe suggested that war is "the needy bankrupt's last resort." Thomas Hobbes said there are three principal causes of war: "competition, diffidence, and glory." But the ancient philosopher, Plato, was probably the closest to the truth when he said, "Wars and factions and fightings have no other source than the body and its lusts. For it is for the getting of wealth that all our wars arise; and we are compelled to get wealth because of our body, to whose service we are slaves."

THE ORIGIN OF CONFLICTS

James asks the very same question. "From whence come wars and fightings among you? Come they not hence, even of your lusts that war in your members [or within you]?" (Ja 4:1).

In the previous chapter we contrasted earthly wisdom with that which is from above. We found that human wisdom is characterized by bitter envying, confusion, and strife. In other words, James is telling us that war reflects the characteristics of earthly wisdom. Earthly wisdom and war go together!

Global war, gang fights, even family quarrels find their origin in lust. James continues by saying, "Ye lust, and have not: ye kill, and desire to have, and cannot obtain: ye fight and war, yet ye have not, because ye ask not" (Ja 4:2).

Edward Gibbon described war as "the chief pursuit of ambitious minds." "It gratifies . . . the combative instinct of mankind," said Charles Eliot, "but it gratifies also the love of plunder, destruction, cruel discipline and arbitrary power." In 1880 the famous Civil War hero, General William T. Sherman, expressed how he felt about armed strife when he stated, "War is hell." War, to be sure, brings out the very worst in man.

Throughout history mankind has repeatedly confirmed the apostle's words, "From whence come wars and fightings among you? . . . even of your lusts" (Ja 4:1). Yes, war—every kind of war—is the result of the evil desires that pollute the mind of man.

"Know thyself," said the ancient philosopher, Socrates. Certainly that is a healthy and commendable suggestion. But according to the prophet Jeremiah, "The heart is deceitful above all things, and desperately wicked: who can know it?" (Jer 17:9). Jeremiah declared that the human nature is desperately evil. It is more wicked than you could ever begin to realize. You cannot imagine what you are capable of.

It is often shocking to witness just how fast people can go to pieces. In a moment of lust, a teenager turns into a thief. Overcome by greed, a respected businessman becomes an embezzler. In a senseless search for excitement, a man or woman sacrifices a good reputation and becomes involved in sexual immorality.

The word *lust* used here by James speaks of unsatisfied desire, literally evil desires. In his letter to young Timothy, Paul tells of the departure of his friend, Demas, "For Demas hath forsaken me, having loved this present world" (2 Ti 4:10). The tug of possessions ruined Paul's companion and fellow servant. The desires of the world drew him away.

The first four chapters of the book of Acts give us the thrilling success story of the early church. We are told of the tremendous growth and victory experienced by that first group of believers. But in chapter 5 we see the beginnings of strife! Barnabas, one of the wealthy members of the church, willingly sold his land and donated the money to the ministry of the apostles.

Luke tells us that a certain man and his wife in the church (Ananias and Sapphira) saw the honor that Barnabas received and lusted after this praise. Selling a piece of their property, they held back part of the money and gave just a portion to the leaders of the church.

In essence, they wanted what Barnabas *had* without doing what he *did*. They were not willing to pay the price!

Human nature is shockingly deceitful. Throughout the Word of God we find the tragic results of human lust. James says it is the lust of power, the lust of personal gain that is the root of all conflict.

Cain lusted after Abel because Abel had found favor with God. King Saul lusted after David because he had found favor with the people of Israel. Their lust welled up within them and resulted in murder and strife.

Abraham Lincoln once walked down the street with his two sons, both of whom were crying. "What's the matter with your boys?" asked a passerby. "Exactly what is wrong with the whole world," said Lincoln. "I have three walnuts, and each boy wants two."

Lust in one form or another is the common sin that plagues all of mankind.

Today in America we are witnessing an ever-growing desire for material possessions. Things which just a short while ago were luxuries are today necessities! We are continually seeking to accumulate things—never satisfied with what we have.

Labor fights with management; workers go on strike. Why? Often it is because of the evil desires and lust of men. The more they have, the more they want.

At the same time big business and management refuse to come to agreements with their workers—often because they too are greedy. Profits never seem big enough. The lust after money becomes an obsession. Wealth is their god.

At the outset of World War II, Hitler defended his acts of aggression by declaring that Germany was simply seeking more "living space."

In her lust for power, Russia has openly declared that Communism will one day conquer the world. North Vietnam seeks to dominate its neighbor to the south. Even the United States defended its early annexation of the west by calling it "manifest destiny."

Throughout history, men and nations have had a lust for power and authority. And James tells us that this evil desire is the cause of war.

I will never forget the speech that was given by General Douglas MacArthur when Japan surrendered at the close of

World War II. Referring to the continuing threat of war, MacArthur declared,

> Military alliance, balances of power, the League of Nations—all in turn have failed. We have had our last chance. If we do not devise some greater and more equitable system, Armageddon will be at our door. The problem basically, is theological and involves a spiritual recrudescence and improvement of human character that will synchronize with our almost matchless advance in science, art, literature, and all material and cultural developments of the past two thousand years. It must be of the *spirit* if we are to save flesh.

THE SOLUTION FOR CONFLICTS

Yes, my friend, the problem of war is theological. Man's basic need today is the need for spiritual birth. He needs a new nature which God alone can impart through His Son, Jesus Christ. The solution begins with the individual. The starting point is the new birth.

In his letter to Christian believers, James makes specific reference to the cause of conflict among those to whom he is writing. He asks, "From whence come wars and fightings among you?" No doubt he is here referring to a problem in the local church. Evidently there was some feuding going on.

It really doesn't make much difference where strife is found. The origin of a family squabble or the cause of a world conflict can both be traced to *selfish lust!*

In his third epistle, the apostle John speaks of a man in the church who so loved attention that he refused to accept the apostle *or* his letters. "I wrote unto the church: but Diotrephes, who loveth to have the preeminence among them, receiveth us not" (3 Jn 9). That man's problem was his lust for position, his desire for authority; and he was causing "war" in the church.

R. V. G. Tasker has said, "Human nature is indeed in the grip of an overwhelming army of occupation. Its natural aim, it can truthfully be said, is pleasure; and when we consider the amount of time, energy, money, interest and enthusiasm that men and women give to the satisfaction of this aim we can appreciate the accuracy of James' diagnosis; and Christians can use it as a reliable yardstick by which to measure the sincerity of their religion. Is God or pleasure the dominant concern of their life?"

What about your desires? What are the priorities and concerns in your life? Is there anything within your life that has brought about strife and division?

STEPS TO RESOLVE CONFLICT

1. *Seek the mind of Christ.* Paul wrote concerning two key women in the church at Philippi, "I beseech Euodias, and beseech Syntyche, that they be of the same mind in the Lord" (Phil 4:2). We can be of one mind as we seek and submit to the mind of Jesus Christ. Thank God, these lusts of ours can be put right. We can be of one mind in Christ. How do we deal with these sources of strife? Paul writes, "It is God which worketh in you both to will and to do of his good pleasure" (Phil 2:13). It is God who can work in us. He alone can give us the right desires and help us to do His will.

2. *Call upon the indwelling Holy Spirit.* We, in ourselves, cannot expect to overcome our evil desires. But we can draw upon the greater power of the One who indwells us. Again, Paul declares, "Reckon ye also yourselves to be dead indeed unto sin, but alive unto God" (Ro 6:11).

Instead of being a slave unto sin, bound by my evil lusts and desires, I am, in Christ Jesus, alive and alert to His desires—His will for my life. Strife is no longer a problem when I commit myself totally to Jesus Christ.

The key to solving conflict is found in affirming God's will. When we do this, our desires become His desires, and then His power becomes our power.

3. *Ask for the glory of God.* James declares, "Ye lust, and have not: ye kill, and desire to have, and cannot obtain: ye fight and war, yet ye have not, because ye ask not. Ye ask, and receive not, because ye ask amiss, that ye may consume it upon your lusts" (Ja 4:2-3).

When you do ask of God, as James says, you don't get what you ask for because you are only trying to satisfy yourself. Your only desire is self-gratification. Many people call upon God as if He were a magic genie, someone to grant their every wish and desire!

The word *consume* that James uses in this verse literally means to spend for oneself. In other words, even when you pray, you ask of God, *only* to realize personal benefit, rather than God's glory. That is why your prayers are not heard. That is why there are divisions and conflicts among you . . . because you seek after your own lusts.

My friend, is there a conflict within you today? Are you troubled by warring and strife? Why not submit to Jesus right now? John says, "This is the confidence that we have in him, that, if we ask anything according to his will, he heareth us" (1 Jn 5:14). He knows your burdens. He knows your conflicts, and He wants to give victory and lasting peace. Amidst the promise of wars and rumors of wars Jesus said, "My peace I give unto you" (Jn 14:27). Although the whole world may be in turmoil, the child of God can rest in the arms of the Prince of Peace.

■ "From whence come wars and fightings among you? come they not hence, even of your lusts that war in your members" (Ja 4:1).

- "Wars and factions and fightings have no other source than the body and its lusts. For it is for the getting of wealth that all our wars arise, and we are compelled to get wealth because of our body, to whose service we are slaves." PLATO

- General Douglas MacArthur declared, "Military alliance, balances of power, the League of Nations—all in turn have failed. We have had our last chance. If we do not devise some greater and more equitable system, Armageddon will be at our door. The problem basically, is theological and involves a spiritual recrudescence and improvement of human character that will synchronize with our almost matchless advance in science, art, literature, and all material and cultural developments of the past two thousand years. It must be of the *spirit* if we are to save flesh."

- The key to solving conflict is found in affirming God's will. When we do this, our desires become God's desires, and then His power becomes our power.

Ye adulterers and adulteresses, know ye not that the friendship of the world is enmity with God? whosoever therefore will be a friend of the world is the enemy of God.

JAMES 4:4

10

Friendship With the World

JAMES 4:4

We are living in an age of moral decay! There's no doubt about that.

Everywhere we look we are confronted with the signs of a perverted, bankrupt society. Pornographic literature, once kept under the drugstore counter, is now brazenly sold on most newsstands. Films depicting every immoral perversion imaginable are shown in thousands of theaters around the world. Even network television programs have been bombarded by corruption and filth. Recently, one of America's leading psychologists stated that "by making violence appear glamorous and exciting, and illicit sex normal . . . [we] are setting the stage for a society based on aggression and irresponsibility."

Yes, we are living in an amoral age!

As awful as this condition is, the evilness of our age should really come as no shock to the student of the Bible. For in God's Word we read, "In the last days perilous times shall come. For men shall be lovers of their own selves, covetous, boasters, proud, blasphemers, disobedient to parents, unthankful, unholy, without natural affection, trucebreakers, false accusers, incontinent, fierce, despisers of those that are good, traitors, heady, highminded, lovers of pleasures more than lovers of God" (2 Ti 3:1-4). The Bible predicts that immorality will continue to increase! In fact, as the final day of God's judgment approaches, mankind will sink deeper and deeper into sin.

But for the child of God it is not enough simply to be aware of this condition. In James 4:4 the writer warns of the dangers of a complacent spirit and an easy attitude toward sin. "Ye adulterers and adulteresses," declares James, "know ye not that the friendship of the world is enmity with God? whosoever, therefore, will be a friend of the world is the enemy of God."

Psychologists tell us that the average individual rarely develops more than two or three close friends throughout his entire life. Generally it is true that a man is known by the friends that he keeps. Who we are, what we do, how we act —all are determined, in part, by those with whom we associate.

James declares that it is impossible to be a friend of the world and of God at the same time. We have a choice to make.

Our Lord, in His parable of the unwise steward, told His disciples that, "No servant can serve two masters: for either he will hate the one, and love the other; or else he will hold to the one, and despise the other. Ye cannot serve God and mammon" (Lk 16:13).

In his book, *A Faith That Works*, B. J. Chitwood suggests that,

> When we become a friend of the world, we take our stand in defiance of God. And, God views it as an act of an enemy, an act of espionage against him. It is as if we were conducting guerrilla warfare against the Lord. We are aiding and abetting the enemy—the same sin committed by Judas. We ask, "How could a man be so black-hearted as to betray Jesus with a kiss of brotherhood?" We are aghast at this most infamous deed in human history. But is that deed

any more treacherous than for us to name the name of Jesus Christ but to serve the camp of the enemy?

At the beginning of chapter 4 James has already stated that all of this world's conflict is the result of lust and fleshly desire. Strife in our homes, conflicts in our business, schools, and churches, even world war finds root in the sinful lusts of men. Here in verse 4 James uses a startling salutation! "Ye adulterers and adulteresses." The allusion James was making was actually quite familiar to his audience. The prophecies of Hosea, Ezekiel, and Isaiah had often pictured the children of Israel as the unfaithful, impure wife of Jehovah. When God's chosen people turned from Jehovah and began to follow after false gods they were, in God's eyes, guilty of spiritual adultery.

Then, too, throughout the Bible Jesus Christ is pictured as the Bridegroom who will one day claim the true church to be His chosen bride. As the bride of Christ, true believers are to keep themselves pure from the "evil and adulterous generation" which Jesus spoke of in Matthew 12:39.

Just as a good husband will not tolerate a rival, neither will Jesus Christ tolerate a division in our affections. You are either for Christ or against Him. James says that friendship with the world means enmity with God.

The first big question we need to ask ourselves is:

WHAT IS THE WORLD?

Surely, in this portion of Scripture, James is not referring to the creative world or the act of God's own hand. Jesus often spoke of the fish of the sea, of birds and flowers, and of all creation. These were things which were made for man. Nor was James speaking of the world of needy people. This is the world that God "so loved," for whom He gave "his only begotten son" to die—that sinful man might be redeemed (Jn 3:16).

No, that is not the world that James was referring to. We must love the people of this confused and calloused world. We are to love a lost world, but we are to be free from the philosophy and practices of this world system.

The apostle John told believers, "Love not the world, neither the things that are in the world. [For] If any man love the world, the love of the Father is not in him" (1 Jn 2:15). Those are strong words!

What kind of world is it that these verses speak of? James speaks of the "system" man has created for himself in which he attempts to live without God. A "man of the world" is a man who is thoroughly caught up and devoted to this kind of living. Worldliness also includes our desire for honor, our struggle for position and recognition. It includes our refusal to be prophetic and our willingness to be used wrongly by this world.

The child of God cannot avoid the fact that he is a citizen of this planet. We are *in* the world—but we are not to be *of* the world. Jesus prayed, "I pray not that thou shouldest take them out of the world, but that thou shouldest keep them from the evil [one]. They are not of the world, even as I am not of the world" (Jn 17:15-16). In other words, the believer in Jesus Christ is different! We are a heavenly people born from above. We are pictured in God's Word as pilgrims, as sojourners just passing through this world.

Paul wrote to the church at Galatia: "Who [Jesus Christ] gave himself for our sins, that he might deliver us from this present evil world, according to the will of God our Father" (Gal 1:4). The reason Jesus came to earth to die, the only purpose of redemption, is that we might be *delivered from the bonds of sin,* that we might be delivered from this evil world. This is the will of God for every believer.

The second question we should consider is:

What is god's attitude toward the world?

James continues on in chapter 4, verse 4 by declaring "Whosoever therefore will be a friend of the world is the enemy of God." A believer who is a friend of the world, one who is motivated by the world's desires and characterized by worldly wisdom, is an *enemy of God!* Did you know that, my friend? Those are not my words. That is not a pronouncement of some church or religious organization. That is a declaration from God's Word.

Now, I realize there are many things in this world that are not deliberately anti-God—things that are not openly defiant of God's laws. But in a very real way many of these seemingly innocent desires and activities are ungodly. Why? Because they retard our spiritual appetite, and they weaken our influence and testimony for Jesus Christ. They compromise our witness. We may cultivate friendships with worldly people who are wonderful, gifted, and charming folks, but who are entirely Godless. In our effort to feel comfortable and accepted by them we may automatically lower our standards to their level of conduct. What is the result? Enmity with God!

James is not saying, don't be friendly toward unbelievers. He is simply saying, even as the apostle Paul said in Romans 12:2, "Don't let the world squeeze you into its own mould" (Phillips). "Be not conformed to this world." James is saying, Be careful in your friendships.

A third question we should consider is:

Does god's word give us any guidelines concerning worldliness?

As we study the Bible, we find many definite commands concerning the believer's standards of behavior. Certain things are always right, and certain things are always wrong.

They are unchangeable even as God's laws are unchangeable. For instance, it is always right to show love and concern for those around you. At the same time it is always wrong to lie or to steal. Certain areas of conduct are predetermined by God's Word.

But between the definite commands concerning good and evil there is an area that presents problems. There is a kind of "no-man's-land" where the absolutes are not so clear. The Bible does not provide a "thou shalt" and a "thou shalt not" for every situation we face day by day.

But in 1 Corinthians 10:23 Paul indicates that even without a yes or no for each situation of life we can know what is right and wrong. Paul says, "All things are lawful for me, but all things are not expedient: all things are lawful for me, but all things edify not."

What is Paul saying? He is saying that there are things which are legitimate—things which are not sinful in and of themselves—but I will avoid them. Why? Because they are out of place in the Christian life. They are unwise. They are unprofitable, and they neither build us up nor edify the Lord Jesus Christ.

Here are four principles which I have found to be of help in determining my activity and actions:

1. *The principle of influence.* Paul wrote to the church at Corinth, "If meat make my brother to offend, I will eat no flesh while the world standeth lest I make my brother to offend" (1 Co 8:13). No man is an island. No one lives to himself. Each one of us, every day of our lives, is influencing those around us either for God or Satan. Paul is saying that if what I eat is distasteful to my brother, then I will not eat it. I can eat it, there is nothing seemingly wrong or evil with it, but I will not do *anything* that would offend those who evaluate the Christian life by what they see in me.

My friend, how about you? Are you a stepping-stone or a

stumbling block to your neighbor? You are an open book, known and read by all who see you. Are you living by the principle of influence?

2. *The principle of ownership.* Again in 1 Corinthians Paul writes, "Know ye not that your body is the temple of the Holy Ghost which is in you, which ye have of God, and ye are not your own? For ye are bought with a price: therefore glorify God in your body, and in your spirit, which are God's" (1 Co 6:19-20).

Anything that we do, any activity that we engage in, must be in keeping with God's claim upon our lives. We are His creation. He *made* us, and He has *redeemed* us. We are twice His.

Oftentimes we hear of the accomplishments of so-called "self-made men." But in reality there is no such thing as a self-made man. The Word of God tells us that "we are his workmanship created in Christ Jesus" (Eph 2:10). He made us, He owns us, and our every action must be in conformity to His will.

3. *The principle of self.* Again to the church at Corinth, Paul declares, "I keep under my body, and bring it into subjection: lest that by any means, when I have preached to others, I myself should be a castaway" (1 Co 9:27).

This principle applies to my effectiveness for Jesus Christ. Paul kept his body under subjection. He wanted to excel. The athlete who wants to be number one must sacrifice at all costs. He must give up everything, good or bad, that would keep him from reaching his goal. What does the Bible say concerning our worldly interests and entanglements? We are told to "lay aside every weight, and the sin which doth so easily beset us, and . . . run with patience the race that is set before us" (Heb 12:1).

I find that there are many Christians today who want to hang onto the world and run the race at the same time. They want to hang onto their favorite sins instead of stripping them away. Before we enter any questionable activity, we should ask ourselves, "What effect will this have on me? Can I honestly ask God's blessing on what I am doing?" Paul said, "I keep my body under subjection at all costs lest that I, having preached to others should myself become a castaway." The word *castaway* that Paul uses here literally means a "disapproved or unfaithful steward," one who fails to meet God's standards.

It is said that, upon coming to the end of his life, the Russian czar, Peter the Great, lamented, "I have conquered an empire but I have not been able to conquer myself." Like so many others, he failed in the greatest test of all—total subjection of oneself to Jesus Christ.

4. *The principle of God's glory.* The most important question we can ask ourselves is, "Will my actions be pleasing to Jesus Christ? If Christ should return right now, would I feel at ease in what I am doing? In other words, would I bring honor to God?" Dr. Robert Cook has said, "The question is not How much may I indulge in and still be saved? God forbid! I must rather ask What about Christ's will and the example I set for my fellow Christians?"

These four principles have no particular magic. They will not provide you with pat answers. But they will give guidance as you honestly seek the Lord's will in your life.

Time after time the Bible reveals God's will concerning this evil world. Paul says in 1 Thessalonians 5:22, "Abstain from all appearance of evil." Keep away from anything that even appears to be bad. "Love not the world," said John, "neither the things that are in the world" (1 Jn 2:15). First and foremost the Christian life is a *positive* allegiance to Jesus Christ. We should become so occupied with Jesus Christ that the things of this world become stale and tasteless.

There is little danger of conforming to the world *without*, if you have enough of Christ *within*.

James puts it very simply—friendship with the world equals enmity with God. It is impossible to share allegiance with two masters. The Christian life is not an easy life. Jesus never gained His disciples under false pretenses. At no time did our Lord promise a bed of roses or a flower-strewn pathway. Nor would we be guilty of that kind of deception today. We want people who love Christ and who are willing to present their bodies as "a living sacrifice, holy, acceptable unto God" (Ro 12:1). C. T. Studd's motto was, "If Jesus Christ be God and died for me, then no sacrifice can be too great for me to make for Him."

My friend, won't you make this the day you yield your life totally and unreservedly to Jesus Christ?

- "Ye adulterers and adulteresses, know ye not that the friendship of the world is enmity with God? whosoever therefore will be a friend of the world is the enemy of God" (Ja 4:4).
- "The question is not How much may I indulge in and still be saved? God forbid! I must rather ask What about Christ's will and the example I set for my fellow Christians?" ROBERT COOK
- We should become so occupied with Jesus Christ that the things of this world become stale and tasteless.
- C. T. Studd's motto was, "If Jesus Christ be God and died for me, then no sacrifice can be too great for me to make for Him."

Go to now, ye that say, To day or to morrow we will go into such a city, and continue there a year, and buy and sell, and get gain:

Whereas ye know not what shall be on the morrow. For what is your life? It is even a vapour, that appeareth for a little time, and then vanisheth away.

For that ye ought to say, If the Lord will, we shall live, and do this, or that.

But now ye rejoice in your boastings: all such rejoicing is evil.

Therefore to him that knoweth to do good, and doeth it not, to him it is sin.

JAMES 4:13-17

11

When a Man Forgets God

JAMES 4:13-17

"What is your life," writes the apostle James. "It is even a vapour, that appeareth for a little time, and then vanisheth away" (Ja 4:14). Yes, life is brief. It is here for a moment and then gone. "Life is so short," someone has said, "that the wood of the cradle rubs up tightly against the marble of the tomb."

Here in chapter 4, James presents a picture of those who lived as if tomorrow would never come. These first century merchants were obsessed with materialism. Buying, selling, and making a profit were their major interests. The accumulation of this world's wealth was their only concern. They had completely forgotten about God and His claim upon their lives.

DON'T FORGET GOD

Many people today, even as in the first century, have forgotten about God. They have decided that religion and business do not mix. Their entire lives are motivated by greed and the desire to make money.

Several years ago the world was shocked to hear of the multimillion dollar business swindle engineered by the likable, church-going Texan, Billie Sol Estes. Typical of thousands of other people in our world today, Estes saw nothing wrong in taking people for whatever he could get out of them.

It seems that ethics in business has gone out of style! Recent statistics show that stealing on the job by employees has skyrocketed! Losses at construction sites alone top 500 million dollars each year. "We simply have to consider theft as a part of the cost of doing business," said one contractor recently. Much of labor and management have accepted the idea that the right to steal is one of the employees' fringe benefits.

A recent article in *Time* magazine illustrates the fact that many of our leading manufacturers today are interested in only one thing—that is making money. Quality of materials, safety regulations, and other important considerations take a back seat to the almighty margin of profit. Yes, leaving God out of business has become the normal thing to do. It is no longer the exception to the rule.

In his letter to Christians, the apostle James states that true religion and one's business *must* mix. One's life and faith must be in total harmony.

Don't be presumptuous

In this passage, James tells us what happens when a man forgets God. "[Come] now, ye that say, to day or to morrow we will go into such a city, and continue there a year, and buy and sell, and get gain" (Ja 4:13). Here James is condemning an attitude of presumption! Wait just a minute, exclaims the apostle, and think about what you are actually doing. He is speaking out against the presumptuous man whose only consideration is making a fast buck and moving on. This, says James, is in contradiction to true Christianity.

A customer once suggested a dishonest transaction to a store clerk saying, "It will be all right, your boss is out." The

clerk, who was a committed Christian, rejected the customer's offer by saying, "My *real* boss is never out!" A true
Christian should be no more inclined to leave God out of his
business affairs than he would be to leave God out of any
other area of his life.

The Bible tells us about a young man who demonstrated
his convictions even in his business affairs. In the book of
Genesis we read that, "the LORD was with Joseph, and he was
a prosperous man." But more than that, we are told that
"his master *saw* that the LORD was with him" (Gen 39:2-3).
Joseph's life was above reproach. But more important, it
demonstrated positive evidence of God's presence with him.

The Bible tells us that Joseph was especially loved by his
father, Jacob. And because of his preferred position he was
greatly envied by his brothers. As a result of this hatred,
Joseph was sold by his brothers into slavery and taken to
Egypt. It was there, in Egypt, that Joseph found himself a
prosperous employee in the house of Potiphar.

While working for Potiphar, Joseph demonstrated two
great characteristics. First, he did his work well. Genesis
39:4 reads, "Joseph found grace in [Potiphar's] sight, and
he served him: and he made him overseer over his house,
and all that he had he put into his hand." Joseph's work was
characterized by excellence, and he was rewarded for it.
What an example to follow! The Christian should seek to
excel! We should always strive to do our very best in business
or in any other area of life.

Second, we read that Joseph was true to God in the hour
of temptation. In Genesis 39:7-9 we read that "it came to
pass after these things, that his master's wife cast her eyes
upon Joseph; and she said, Lie with me. But he refused, and
said unto his master's wife, Behold, my master wotteth not
what is with me in the house, and he hath committed all that
he hath to my hand; there is none greater in this house than I;

neither hath he kept back any thing from me but thee, because thou art his wife: how then can I do this great wickedness, and sin against God?"

Joseph was true to God even in the hour of temptation. Oh yes, he suffered for it. He was unjustly accused and even thrown into prison. But in the end he was elevated to an even greater position of authority. God was with him. He delivered him and honored his faithfulness.

My friend, you never do right by doing wrong. James and Joseph both tell us, "Do not leave God out of your life's work." Make Jesus Christ the center of your vocation.

As we examine this portion of James' epistle, we see several excellent principles set forth by the apostle. First of all, James is saying, "Do not be presumptuous with God. Do not leave God out of your plans for tomorrow; do not forget about God! Why? Simply because you do not know what tomorrow will bring.

Don't count on tomorrow

In verse 14 we read that "ye know not what shall be on the morrow." Yesterday is gone. Tomorrow is uncertain. Therefore, live for Jesus Christ today!

In the book of Ruth, Naomi asked of her daughter-in-law, "Where hast thou gleaned to day?" (Ruth 2:19). What about you? What have you accomplished for Jesus Christ today? Jesus' words to Zaccheus were, "To day I must abide at thy house" (Lk 19:5). Now is the accepted time. Live for Christ today! We know not what a day may bring forth. Yield your entire life this day to the Lord.

Jesus once told a parable of a rich man who thought only of himself. One year he had such a bountiful harvest that he had no place to store all his crops. Jesus said that this man "thought within himself, saying, What shall I do, because I have no room where to bestow my fruits? And he said, This will I do: I will pull down my barns, and build greater; and there will I bestow all my fruits and my goods. And I will say to my soul, Soul, thou hast much goods laid up for many years; take thine ease, eat, drink, and be merry." What arrogance! What presumption!

But God said unto him, "Thou fool, this night thy soul shall be required of thee" (Lk 12:17-20). In a moment he was stripped of everything. He was totally dispossessed!

My friend, do not count on tomorrow, for you know not what tomorrow may bring.

Many people today, like this rich fool, are only concerned about material things. We find that in the United States, per capita income has increased 89 percent in the last ten years. Even after inflation is considered, we are taking home 42 percent more in wages than we did a decade ago. One in three American families now owns a second car, nearly half own at least one color television set, one-third of all our households own freezers, 20 percent now have automatic dishwashers. More and more families are purchasing second homes in the country—affluence abounds! "Eat, drink, and be merry," has become a national motto.

Oh, the dangers, my friend, when men forget God. James reminds us that life is short, "For what is your life? It is even a vapour, that appeareth for a little time, and then vanisheth away" (Ja 4:14b). The word *vapor* used here is the same word that is often used for smoke—that which is here one moment and gone the next.

In his play, *MacBeth*, Shakespeare pictures the brevity of life:

> Out, out, brief candle!
> Life's but a walking shadow, a poor player
> That struts and frets his hour upon the stage
> And then is heard no more. It is a tale
> Told by an idiot, full of sound and fury,
> Signifying nothing.

Edward Young pictured life as nothing but "bubbles on the rapid stream of time."

It is true that man's life expectancy has risen dramatically during this century. In parts of the world an average lifespan now exceeds seventy years. But in reality whether a man lives to be thirty, fifty, or even one hundred years, his time is still but a wisp of vapor that appears for a moment and then vanishes. I never cease to be amazed at the numbers of people who spend an entire lifetime attempting to accumulate enough wealth so that they will be able to one day retire and live a life of ease. Oftentimes they literally kill themselves amassing earthly wealth that they never get a chance to enjoy. And the treasures that they should have been concerned about—heavenly treasures—they completely ignore. Jesus said, "Lay not up for yourselves treasures upon earth, where moth and rust doth corrupt, and where thieves break through and steal: but lay up for yourselves treasures in heaven, where neither moth nor rust doth corrupt, and where thieves do not break through nor steal: for where your treasure is, there will your heart be also" (Mt 6:19-21).

What is your life? Have you tasted of the real, meaningful life that Jesus came to bring? Or is your existence full of "sound and fury, signifying nothing." Jesus said, "I am come that they might have life, and that they might have it more abundantly" (Jn 10:10). He wants to give you fullness. A realization of the brevity of life should lead you to a full-hearted trust in Jesus Christ. Real life—eternal life—begins when you receive Jesus Christ as Saviour and Lord.

James, of course, is not suggesting that our physical life is unimportant, nor is he writing against a well-planned life. But he *is* warning us about a presumptuous spirit and the brevity of life.

Finally, James teaches that everything should be subject to the will of God. In verse 15 James says, "You ought to say,

If the Lord will, we shall live, and do this, or that." A man who is living in the will of God is a man who is ready for anything.

Someone once asked the great evangelist, George White-field, what he would do if he knew Jesus Christ would return in just three days. Whitefield produced his date book and said, "I would do just what I have scheduled to do." He was confidently living *in* God's will.

Notice our *duty* that James speaks of in verse 15. "You *ought* to say, if the Lord wills." *Ought* signifies duty. All of our living should be in the light of God's will.

These businessmen of whom James is writing were not only being presumptuous with God, they were literally taking their lives into their own hands. They were assuming that they were in full control of their own destinies. They had their entire future mapped out. They were in the driver's seat, handling the controls. Seemingly, they had no idea that God might have other plans for them.

In many respects, this kind of attitude places a man in total rebellion against God. For in the very act of ordering his own future, he refuses to acknowledge God's power and right to interpose His will in us. James declares that it is much better to say, "If God wills, I will do thus and so."

A. B. Simpson once said, "I like to interpose in all of my appointments, if the Lord wills." James here is speaking about attitude. "If God wills," is not just a trite phrase or a neat formula. No, it is an indication of an attitude of complete submission to God. Our heavenly Father should be our partner in all our plans.

The great preacher, Dr. George Truett, used to say: "*To know* the will of God is the greatest knowledge! *To do* the will of God is the greatest achievement!"

My friend, do not leave God out of your plans. Do not try to run your own life according to your own blueprint. Jesus declared, "Seek ye the kingdom of God; and all these things shall be added unto you" (Lk 12:31). Accept His kingship and domain, and everything else will fall into place.

Many people are never willing to acknowledge Christ in their lives until they come to a period of suffering. Surely all of our hard times and trouble are not a result of sin. But God *does* deal firmly with us at times so that we might become pliable and willing to seek His perfect will.

I recall a young attractive couple who were alert and capable, but who resolutely refused to yield to the will of God. They completely neglected God as they lived totally unto themselves. Before long God permitted difficulties to enter their lives. One of their sons became ill and had to be hospitalized. A short time later the wife suffered a nervous breakdown. And minor things happened—the washing machine broke down, the furnace stopped working. Their problems steadily multiplied.

This was obviously beyond the natural. The hand of God was working in their home, seeking to bring them to submission. Soon they yielded their lives totally to Jesus Christ. They sought *His* will, and let *Him* take control.

That is the solution! Do not try to go it alone.

The Bible says, "Trust in the LORD with all thine heart; and lean not unto thine own understanding. In all thy ways acknowledge him, and he shall direct thy paths" (Pro 3:5-6). My friend, have you acknowledge Jesus Christ as Saviour? As Lord?

James warns us: Do not forget God! Do not be presumptuous! Do not count on tomorrow! Do not leave Jesus Christ out of your life, and do not delay.

James concludes this chapter by saying, "Therefore to him that knoweth to do good, and doeth it not, to him it is sin" (Ja 4:17). Knowledge brings responsibility.

- "For that ye ought to say, If the Lord will, we shall live, and do this, or that" (Ja 4:15).

- Do not forget God! Do not be presumptuous! Do not count on tomorrow. Do not leave Jesus Christ out of your life, and do not delay!

- My *real boss* is never out.

- "I like to interpose in all of my appointments, if the Lord wills." A. B. SIMPSON

- "*To know* the will of God is the greatest knowledge! *To do* the will of God is the greatest achievement." GEORGE TRUETT

Go to now, ye rich men, weep and howl for your miseries that shall come upon you.

Your riches are corrupted, and your garments are moth-eaten.

Your gold and silver is cankered; and the rust of them shall be a witness against you, and shall eat your flesh as it were fire. Ye have heaped treasure together for the last days.

Behold, the hire of the labourers who have reaped down your fields, which is of you kept back by fraud, crieth: and the cries of them which have reaped are entered into the ears of the Lord of sabaoth.

Ye have lived in pleasure on the earth, and been wanton; ye have nourished your hearts, as in a day of slaughter.

Ye have condemned and killed the just; and he doth not resist you.

JAMES 5:1-6

12

Your Money: A Blessing or Curse?

Many people today feel that money is the key to happiness. "If only I had more money," they say, "I would really be happy."

But as we look around us we find that things do not usually work out that way. The more money we have, the more we need—and the more we make, the more we spend. Someone has described money as simply "a device which permits people to get into debt a little farther."

Is money the key to everything? Can money bring solutions to all of life's problems? James C. Hefley relates the effect money has had upon some of the world's richest men. In 1923 a group of seven financial giants gathered together at the Edgewater Beach Hotel in Chicago. Their combined wealth totaled more than the worth of the United States Treasury. For years these men had been admired and respected as examples of success and prosperity. But, twenty-five years later, a check was made. Charles Schwab, president of the largest independent steel company, had died penniless. Arthur Cutten, millionaire wheat speculator, had met the same disappointing end. Richard Whitney, president of the New York Stock Exchange, had served several years in prison. Albert Fall, a member of the presidential cabinet, had been pardoned from prison so he could die at home. Jesse Livermore, the greatest "bear" on Wall Street, had committed suicide. Leon Fraser, the president of the Bank of International Settlement, had committed suicide. Ivan Krueger, head of the world's greatest monopoly, also had taken his own life.

With all of their wealth and power, these men had not found happiness or lasting peace. Money can be a great blessing, but it can also be a terrible curse.

I suppose that money is one of the most popular subjects today—and in many ways it is a very serious topic of discussion. Money, or the lack of money, does terrible things to people. Millions of people in our world starve to death every year simply because they did not have enough money to buy food. On the other hand, there are people who have *more* money than they can possibly use. And yet they, too, are starving—starving for fulfillment and meaning in life. The *Wall Street Journal,* a paper devoted to the discussion of finance, described money as "an article which may be used as a universal passport to everywhere except Heaven, and as a universal provider of everything except happiness."

There is nothing wrong with being wealthy. The Bible does not condemn riches! Joseph of Arimathaea must have been rich to own the new tomb which he gave for the burial of our Lord. Barnabas, a leader in the early church, was a wealthy man who used his money for the Lord's work. Abraham was a man of faith and a friend of God, but he was also very rich. Solomon is described in the Bible as one of the wealthiest men of his day. There is no harm in possessing riches, but in letting riches possess you.

In chapter 5 of this epistle, James speaks to those who let money become their God: "[Come] now, ye rich men, weep and howl for your miseries that shall come upon you. Your riches are corrupted, and your garments are motheaten. Your gold and silver is cankered; and the rust of them shall be a witness against you, and shall eat your flesh as it were fire. Ye have heaped treasure together for the last days" (Ja 5:1-3). These rich men, against whom James was speaking, had become corrupted by their wealth. James points out how foolish it is to put high value upon riches, to work feverishly at amassing great wealth. But at the same time the apostle is attempting to impress upon those who were believers, the great threat that riches can be to the child of God. Wealth can so easily eat away like a canker, and make us lose our sense of priorities.

This was the sin of the rich young ruler in Mark 10. We are told that when this young man who had "great possessions" came to Jesus for spiritual advice, Jesus told him to give away his wealth for he had become a slave to his money.

In His Sermon on the Mount, Jesus warned the disciples concerning the transitory nature of wealth. "Lay not up for yourselves treasures upon earth, where moth and rust doth corrupt, and where thieves break through and steal: but lay up for yourselves treasures in heaven, where neither moth nor rust doth corrupt, and where thieves do not break through nor steal: for where your treasure is, there will your heart be also" (Mt 6:19-21). Money is deceiving for it brings a false sense of security. Paul warned Timothy that "they that will be rich fall into temptation and a snare, and into many foolish and hurtful lusts, which drown men in destruction and perdition. For the love of money is the root of all evil: which while some coveted after, they have erred from the faith, and pierced themselves through with many sorrows" (1 Ti 6:9-10). Beware of the deceitfulness of money.

UNUSED MONEY

The men to whom James addresses himself here in chapter 5 had hoarded their riches. They were counting on all their prosperity to keep them happy. They were not using their money for any worthwhile purpose. James warns of the subtle sinfulness of idle wealth. The Dead Sea is a dead sea because it takes everything in and gives nothing out. The law of living is giving. If money is to be useful, it must be used.

In Bible times riches consisted of beautiful clothing and precious metal. Immense value resided in garments passed down from generation to generation. Jacob gave Joseph a coat of many colors. Joseph gave Benjamin five changes of raiment. Samson promised thirty changes of garments to the one who guessed his riddle. It was very common to place a great deal of importance in clothing. James said to the rich men who had hoarded up clothing and wealth, "Your riches are corrupted, and your garments are motheaten" (Ja 5:2). In other words, "Your wealth will get you nowhere." It is temporal.

The problem here was *unused* money. These men had gathered riches for riches sake. James said, "The rust of them [your wealth] shall be a witness against you" (Ja 5:3). Rust is a symbol of disuse. It is a sign of inactivity. Henry Ford used to say, "Money is just like an arm or a leg—you either use it or lose it." To make money you have to spend it.

It is also true that money unused will never help to spread the gospel. One of the bottlenecks of world evangelization is money. Money unused will never supply the needs of missions; it will never feed and clothe the hungry and naked. To be blessed with wealth and not use it is sinful. James says, "[It] shall be a witness against you" (Ja 5:3). Unused money will accuse you of poor stewardship in the judgment day.

God endows some of His children with a special ability to make money. But all of us can give Him back a portion of that with which He has blessed us. There is so much that God's people *can* do with *His* money. There is really too much to do! Look at your own situation. Financially speaking, are you losing what you are not using?

Henry Crowell, founder of the Quaker Oats Company and one of the significant contributors to the work of the Moody Bible Institute, was a man who knew how to *use* his money. As a young man, he accepted Jesus Christ as his Saviour. When he began his business career in a little Ohio factory, he promised God that he would honor Him in his giving. God's blessing was upon young Crowell. As his business grew, he increased his giving. After decades of faithful stewardship, Crowell testified, "For over forty years I have given 60 or 70 percent of my income to God, but I've never gotten ahead of God. He has always been ahead of me in giving." Crowell knew how to use His money wisely!

DIRTY MONEY

Not only were the rich men in this epistle guilty of hoarding away their money, but James also condemns them because their wealth was tainted. These men had held back wages from their employees. James says that they had cheated their workers out of their pay. Instead of being just with their money, these men spent their money on themselves, satisfying their every whim. The wealth they had not hoarded was squandered on self and on the body. James declares, "Behold, the hire of the labourers who have reaped down your fields, which is of you kept back by fraud, crieth: and the cries of them who have reaped are entered into the ears of the Lord of sabaoth" (Ja 5:4). James is simply saying that God hears the cry of the laborer who has been cheated. He is aware of the injustice you have done, and He will hold you responsible.

In the book of Exodus, God's people Israel were being exploited by the Egyptians. In chapter 3 we read the words of the Lord: "I have surely seen the affliction of my people which are in Egypt, and I have heard their cry by reason of their task masters; for I know their sorrows" (Ex 3:7). Because of Egypt's sin God brought great judgment upon them, and Israel was delivered from their oppression. Yes, God does see. He knows when we fail to use our resources justly, and He judges accordingly. How do you use the money God has given you? Are you a faithful steward or are you guilty of self-indulgence?

Keith Nicholson was a $56-a-week mine worker when he won over $400,000 in the British soccer pool. His wife, who had never had much money before, announced immediately that they were going to "spend, spend, spend." The Nicholsons then proceeded to buy a $47,000 house, two cars, and two television sets. They began to give parties nearly every night. Before long they had spent almost half of their new-found wealth. "We had oodles of money," reported Mrs. Nicholson, "and we set the place alight, but we lost our friends. The people we had known in the old days . . . never come along." The Nicholsons lost their wealth because of their self-indulgence.

Actually, the way we use our money, over and above the needs of life, reveals our true interests. Why not ask yourself, "How do *I* use my assets?" The man who picks up the newspaper and immediately turns to the financial page probably has his money tied up in stocks and bonds. A woman's large annual expenditures for clothes reveals a strong interest in personal appearance. It is true—where your dollars go, that is where your interests lie.

A friend of mine who gives generously to the work of missions was recently asked by the Internal Revenue Service to report to their local office. When questioned about the large sums he reported as contributions, my friend produced his cancelled checks as proof of his giving. The agent reviewed the checks; and, when he was finally convinced that this man actually did give all the money he claimed to have given, he looked at him and said, "Sir, you certainly must be sold on your church." This is a man whose interests are in the right place.

Jesus said, "Where your treasure is, there will your heart be also" (Mt 6:21). There is nothing wrong with legitimate pleasure. All of us enjoy a good time. But James describes rich men who literally immersed themselves in self-indulgent pleasure. They hoarded their wealth, not for a rainy day, not to help others, but purely for their own selfish gratification.

RUTHLESS MONEY

James declares, "Ye have lived in pleasure on the earth, and have been wanton; ye have nourished your hearts, as in a day of slaughter. Ye have condemned and killed the just" (Ja 5: 5-6). Not only were these men guilty of self-centeredness, but they were ruthless in the way they accumulated their wealth. They let nothing and no one stand in their way.

In that day the wealthy had influence in the courts and were able even to condemn to death those who might hinder their greedy goals. Yes, then even as today, money could elevate or lower, enrich or impoverish, bless or blast. Money can bribe, it can seduce, it can poison or damn. But money can also teach and heal. It can help win people to Jesus Christ.

Many people feel that if they give what they have to God in the way of money, they will wind up on the short end of things. Nothing is farther from the truth. These people are like the beggar in the Orient who was sitting by the roadside with his small bowl of rice when a very well dressed prince approached him and asked if he would please share his food. The rebellious beggar protested, but finally grudgingly held out his bowl. As soon as the prince had extracted one grain of rice, the shallow container was quickly withdrawn.

Again the request was made and, after much persuasion, the beggar extended his dish, but pulled it back so rapidly that the prince managed to snare only one additional grain. The wealthy man moved on while the beggar ate the rest of his scanty fare. At the bottom of the bowl, however, he discovered two golden grains of rice which the regal dignitary had given him in exchange. If only the beggar would have given him his all.

Your money will accomplish only what you want it to accomplish. Your money can be an angel to reach thousands for Jesus Christ. Your money can teach the needy, it can help the oppressed. Or it can be a devil. It can be idle, dirty, selfish, and ruthless.

May we dedicate our money this day to Jesus Christ. The opportunities which lie before us are staggering. The needs are vast. If the entire population of the world could be compressed into a single town of 1,000, over 700 would be poor, sick, and hungry. Over 500 would never have heard that Jesus Christ lived and died for their sin. The needs truly are great.

My friend, what are you doing with your money? It is not what we grab, but what we *give* that makes us rich. Determine today to give not just your money, but your entire self to the service of Jesus Christ. He will shower His blessing upon you as you have never known it before.

The time to give is now!

■ "I speak not by commandment, but by occasion of the forwardness of others, and to prove the sincerity of your love. For ye know the grace of our Lord Jesus Christ, that, though he was rich, yet for your sakes he became poor, that ye through his poverty might be rich" (1 Co 8:8-9).

- "Money is just like an arm or a leg—you either use it or lose it." HENRY FORD

- The Dead Sea is a dead sea because it takes everything in and gives nothing out.

- The way we use our money, over and above the needs of life, reveals our true interests.

- "For where your treasure is, there will your heart be also" (Mt 6:2).

Be patient therefore, brethren, unto the coming of the Lord. Behold, the husbandman waiteth for the precious fruit of the earth, and hath long patience for it, until he receive the early and latter rain.

Be ye also patient; stablish your hearts: for the coming of the Lord draweth nigh.

Grudge not one against another, brethren, lest ye be condemned: behold, the judge standeth before the door.

Take, my brethren, the prophets, who have spoken in the name of the Lord, for an example of suffering affliction, and of patience.

Behold, we count them happy which endure. Ye have heard of the patience of Job, and have seen the end of the Lord; that the Lord is very pitiful, and of tender mercy.

JAMES 5:7-11

13

Patience Amid Conflicts

JAMES 5:7-11

"Patience overcomes everything," says the ancient proverb. "The world is his who has patience." For most of us patience is a scarce commodity. But to the Christians of the first century, plagued with problems and intense persecution, patience was more than just a virtue—it was an absolute necessity!

Knowing that the *outlook* was desperately dark, James encouraged these believers to try the *uplook*. "Be patient . . . unto the coming of the Lord" (Ja 5:7). Why be patient? Because God is in control, and He will one day return to receive His own.

There are many things in life which try our patience. All of us experience frustrating moments when we find it difficult to cope with the pressures and problems of life.

To these same believers of the early church who were experiencing severe testings and temptations, the apostle James wrote, "Count it all joy when ye fall into various trials, [for you know] that the testing of your faith worketh patience" (Ja 1:2-3, NSRB*). There is a purpose in testing! There is a reason why we are given difficult experiences—that we might develop patience.

---

*New Scofield Reference Bible

We need patience in every area of life. Driving down the expressway, waiting in line at the supermarket, getting along with that cantankerous person in the office—everything we do requires a degree of patience. Not only do we need patience in our relationships with one another, but we also need patience in our relationship with our heavenly Father.

The great New England preacher, Phillips Brooks, was known for his calmness and poise. His intimate friends, however, knew that he too suffered moments of frustration and irritability. One day a friend saw him pacing the floor like a caged lion. "What is the trouble, Dr. Brooks?" asked the friend. "The trouble is," replied Brooks, "that I'm in a hurry, but God isn't." Have you ever felt that way?

God works in mysterious ways His wonders to perform. Oftentimes *His* timetable is not the same as *ours*. The great theologian and preacher, Andrew Murray, declared, "Be assured that, if God waits longer than you could wish, it is only to make the blessing doubly precious! God waited four thousand years, till the fullness of time, ere He sent His Son. Our times are in His hands; He will avenge His elect speedily; He will make haste for our help, and not delay one hour too long."

Some of the early Christians to whom James was writing were so eager for the second coming of Jesus Christ that they had become impatient for His return. They were beginning to crack under the pressures of persecution. They were beginning to question whether their suffering was worthwhile.

The word used in James 5:7 for *patience* could be better translated "steadfastness" or "endurance." It suggests not so much the idea of resignation to one's fate as the quality of self-restraint. It indicates the need to refrain from striking back at the tempter. Be patient, says James, without seeking revenge. No matter how severe the testing may be, we are to stand firm, take heart, and be patient.

Why were these words of advice given? As we study this passage, we find that James suggests two primary reasons for being patient.

BE PATIENT, BECAUSE JESUS IS COMING

Most of us know what it is like to be away from our home and loved ones for awhile. Think back to that day when you first set out on your own, when you left your friends and family for the first time. It was a hard and lonely experience. But then one day you were able to go home for a visit. You once again had the opportunity of being with those you loved. It was such a wonderful feeling. It was a happy experience.

The return of Jesus Christ to receive His own is called that "blessed hope" or that "happy hope." It will be a time of beautiful reunion, a time when we forever will be united with our heavenly Father. Therefore, says James, "be patient . . . unto the coming of the Lord" (Ja 5:7).

The return of Jesus Christ will usher in a time of uninterrupted fellowship, eternal fellowship with our Lord. Our lives here on earth are often marked by separations. Some of you have been separated from your children by the physical limitations of the body, an undeveloped mind, a lack of hearing or vision, the inability to speak. Some of you already have laid your children to rest. Many, because of death, have been separated from a husband or wife. Life is a series of separations.

For those to whom James was writing, separation was very real. The physical and economic persecution that these Christians had experienced had resulted in the disruption of many families. For some, the pain and suffering was too much to accept.

But to believers of the first century and twentieth century alike, James' words ring out loud and clear: "Be . . . patient;

stablish your hearts: for the coming of the Lord draweth nigh" (Ja 5:8). On that day when Christ returns we will enjoy eternal, unbroken fellowship, "For the Lord himself shall descend from heaven with a shout, with the voice of the archangel, and with the trump of God: and the dead in Christ shall rise first: then we which are alive and remain shall be caught up together with them in the clouds, to meet the Lord in the air: and so shall we ever be with the Lord" (1 Th 4:16-17). There will be no more separation, no more sorrow, for these things shall all pass away. And as the apostle Paul wrote those words to the church at Thessalonica, he concluded by saying, "Wherefore comfort one another with these words" (1 Th 4:18). Despite the sorrow of separation here, we do have that "blessed hope" of unending fellowship when Christ returns.

Yes, we are to be patient for a very important reason—Christ shall return! And when He does come back to catch up His church we will not only enjoy unending fellowship, but, the Bible says, we shall be given a new and glorious body. We shall be changed—in a moment—and have no more sickness and suffering, no more pain, and no more death. John declared that when Christ appears, "we shall be like him; for we shall see him as he is" (1 Jn 3:2). What a day that will be!

Life is filled with conflicts! Every day we are faced with the travesty of war, the ravages of disease, the suffering of those who have nothing to eat. Earthquakes, floods, and fire cause untold hardship. But one day, that great day, these torturing conflicts of life will be straightened out forever.

> If we could see beyond today, as God can see,
> If all the clouds should roll away, the shadows flee;
> O'er present griefs we would not fret,
> Each sorrow we would soon forget;
> For many joys are waiting yet for you and me.

"If we could see, if we could know," we often say.
But God in love a veil doth throw across our way.
We cannot see what lies before
And so we cling to Him the more,
He leads us till this life is o'er;
Trust and obey.

ANONYMOUS

Yes, trust and obey. "Be patient," says James, "for the coming of the Lord draweth nigh." The truth of the coming of Jesus Christ is a great cure for conflict. If the outlook is dark, try the uplook. We need to live in the glow of His coming.

BE PATIENT, BECAUSE GOD IS WORKING

In verse 7 of this chapter, James gives an illustration of the kind of patience we are to possess. "Behold, the husbandman waiteth for the precious fruit of the earth, and hath long patience for it, until he receive the early and latter rain."

The husbandman, or farmer, must patiently wait for the results of his sweat and toil. In the spring he plows, plants, cultivates, and harrows. Patiently day by day, week by week, and month by month he toils over his plants, waiting in expectancy of the harvest which is come. He cannot alter the growing season. He cannot intervene in the natural course of events. He must have patience and wait upon the earth to bring forth her abundance.

In much the same way the Christian must patiently wait upon God to bring about a harvest of character in his life. God is at work. In chapter 1 of this same epistle we read that we are to "let patience have her perfect work, that [we] may be perfect and entire, wanting nothing" (Ja 1:4). "Ye are God's husbandry," Paul wrote to the church at Corinth (1 Co 3:9). We are God's garden, purchased by His precious blood. We have been planted and cultivated by the Lord. And as

God is patiently waiting for fruit in our lives, so we are to patiently wait upon Him to accomplish His purpose.

The husbandman, or farmer, can prepare the ground and plant the seed, but he is totally dependent upon the elements for the growth of his plants. James speaks of the great patience the farmer must have as he waits for the "early and latter rain" (Ja 5:7). In Palestine there are two seasons in the year: a wet season from October to April and a dry season from May to September. The rainy season is absolutely necessary to the farmer, for without the needed moisture there will be no crop to harvest during the long, hot summer.

The same could be said of the human soul. At times the experiences of life can be very hard. If our lives were filled with sunshine only, we would be nothing more than a parched and arid desert. We *need* the storms, for they bring the moisture which produces living things. In all the trying and perplexing experiences of life, God is at work.

The poet had this in mind when he wrote these words:

> Did the leaves of the trees say something to you as you
>   passed them today?
> They were not created this spring but months ago. (And
>   right now others are being fashioned for another year.)
> At the bottom of every leaf stem is a cradle, and in it
>   is an infant germ:
> The winds will rock it and the birds will sing to it all
>   summer long and next spring it will unfold.
>
> AUTHOR UNKNOWN

So God is working in you, "Both to will and to do of his good pleasure" (Phil 2:13). Good days and bad days, sad days and glad days, God is accomplishing His perfect will. The apostle Paul wrote to the church at Rome, "All things work together for good to them that love God, to them who are the called according to his purpose" (Ro 8:28). Therefore, be patient as you wait upon the Lord.

But there is another reason we are to be patient. In verse 9 of this chapter James writes, "Grudge not one against another, brethren, lest ye be condemned: behold, the judge standeth before the door." The coming of Christ will be a happy event, but it will also be a solemn occasion. Therefore, says James, live patiently because "the judge standeth before the door." Jesus Christ is coming to right the wrongs.

Jesus Christ was born to be the Saviour of the world. That was His purpose for coming to this earth, for His death on the cross, and His resurrection from the grave. But if Jesus Christ is rejected and spurned He becomes, not our Saviour, but our eternal Judge. Just as a citizen of this world must abide by certain physical and civil laws, so, too, must he recognize God's spiritual laws. The apostle Paul indicates that there will come a day when every person will have to give an account of himself before God. Paul writes, "But why dost thou judge thy brother? or why dost thou set at nought thy brother? For we shall all stand before the judgment seat of Christ" (Ro 14:10). Again Paul writes that when Christ returns, "Every man's work shall be made manifest . . . and the fire shall try every man's work of what sort it is" (1 Co 3:13). There *will be* a day of reckoning in which our true values shall be revealed.

During the days of persecution and suffering, the early Christians found it easy to blame one another for their problems. In these words of admonition James is simply saying, "Be patient with one another. Do not grumble and complain at your brother because of the problems you are facing. For in so doing you stand in danger of God's own judgment." God's judgment will take strict account of the Christian's behavior as well as that of their persecutors. What! Falling out with one another, when the Judge is standing at the very door!

How sad it is to see children of God who cannot live peaceably with one another. How God's Spirit must be grieved when we grumble and complain instead of being about our Master's work. The time is short! The days are few! The thought of Christ's return is a warning as well as a consolation to each one of us.

Do not groan against your brother, dear Christian. Do not moan about your troubles. Be patient, be happy, whatever your situation might be. Anyone can praise God when everything is going well. Anyone can be joyful when the bank account is full and there is no sickness. The true test of our patience and maturity comes when we find ourselves in a difficult situation, when we are in a jam!

Paul does not say, "If you are so disposed let me suggest that you rejoice." No! He does not say, "Moan with me," or "Groan with me." He says, "Rejoice in the Lord alway: and again I say, Rejoice" (Phil 4:4). No matter what your situation in life may be, no matter what your trial or affliction, wait patiently and rejoice in the Lord! Paul was not merely mouthing sweet-sounding platitudes. These words were spoken as he awaited a martyr's death. Paul knew what it meant to wait patiently upon God in the hour of conflict. Sometimes we sing the words of the hymn writer, Johnson Oatman, Jr.:

> So, amid the conflict, whether great or small,
> Do not be discouraged, God is over all;
> Count your many blessings, angels will attend,
> Help and comfort give you to your journey's end.

Why should the Christian be patient? First, be patient, because "the coming of the Lord draweth nigh." That is our blessed hope, our joy and rejoicing. Second, live patiently because God is at work. And third, practice patience because "the judge standeth before the door."

- "Be ye also patient; stablish your hearts: for the coming of the Lord draweth nigh" (Ja 5:8).
- The truth of the coming of Jesus Christ is a great cure for conflict. Let us live in the glow of His coming.
- The true test of our maturity comes when we find ourselves in a difficult situation, when we are in a jam!
- If the outlook is dark, try the uplook.

Is any among you afflicted? let him pray. Is any merry? let him sing psalms.

Is any sick among you? let him call for the elders of the church; and let them pray over him, anointing him with oil in the name of the Lord:

And the prayer of faith shall save the sick, and the Lord shall raise him up; and if he have committed sins, they shall be forgiven him.

JAMES 5:13-15

14

Divine Healing

JAMES 5:13-15

Oftentimes in the midst of the troubles and turmoils of life, we find ourselves asking, "Does God really care what happens to me?"

Physical or mental illness is common to all of us. It affects each of our lives in one way or another. Why does God permit His children to suffer? Is illness necessary? Can God heal? Does God heal today? Is it always God's will to heal?

Here in the epistle of James we find that God does care about us. He is interested in meeting our needs. James tells us that it is God who "giveth to all men liberally" (Ja 1:5). If any man has need, says James, "let him ask of God." God is all-loving. He is all-powerful, all-wise, and He wants the very best for His children. God does care about me!

In James 5 we find that God is *particularly* concerned about our emotional and physical well-being. In verse 13 we read, "Is any among you afflicted? let him pray. Is any merry? let him sing psalms." What are we to do with our great emotional conflicts in life? James tells us to relate them to God! Whatever else we do we are to pray—to share our emotions with God.

The word *afflicted* used here by James refers to the difficult experiences of life, the depression we experience during times

145

of misfortune. Is any among you suffering? says James, Let him pray. Let him talk it over with God who hears and answers our concerns.

Sometimes the problems of life seem too hard to bear. As a result of our grief, we do not know where to turn or what to do. In Matthew 14 we are told of just such an experience. Here we are given the account of the murder of John the Baptist. Matthew tells us that after John was beheaded, "his head was brought on a charger, and given to the damsel: and she brought it to her mother. And his disciples came, and took up the body, and buried it, and went and told Jesus" (Mt 14:11-12). What a shocking experience! John's disciples were bereft and confused. What were they to do? They picked up his body, buried it, and went and told Jesus of the tragedy. Yes, sorrow comes to all of us. But we, too, can turn to Jesus in our.hour of grief. He understands our sorrow. Isaiah described our Lord as, "a man of sorrows, and acquainted with grief" (Is 53:3). Jesus knew what it was like to be weary. He had no place to lay His head. He knew what it was to be lonely, what it was to suffer. Yes, my friend, we have an Intercessor who is concerned about us when we are distressed.

But there are also glad days. Gladness is a blessed emotion. James declares, "Is any merry? let him sing psalms" (Ja 5:13). Happy or sad, dejected or cheerful, James says to share it with God in prayer. Praise is just as much a part of prayer as are requests. The word *praise* in its various forms is found 550 times in the Bible. Paul told the believers at Philippi to "Rejoice in the Lord alway: and again I say, Rejoice" (Phil 4:4). Praise ought to be our life-style.

Not only do we find prayer to be the solution to the needs of our emotions, but the answer to our physical needs as well. "Is any sick among you? let him call for the elders of the church; and let them pray over him, anointing him with oil in the name of the Lord: and the prayer of faith shall save the sick, and the Lord shall raise him up; and if he have committed sins, they shall be forgiven him" (Ja 5:14-15).

First, notice what is *not* taught here. All sickness is not a direct result of sin. The word *if* in verse 15 clearly suggests that the earlier portion of this verse bears no relation of suffering to sin. James says, "*If* he have committed sins, they shall be forgiven him" (Ja 5:15, italics added). Some sickness *is* a result of sin, and some sickness *is not* a result of sin.

As we study the gospels, we find that even Jesus' disciples were confused about this matter. In John 9:2-3 we read that Jesus' "disciples asked him, saying, Master, who did sin, this man, or his parents, that he was born blind? Jesus answered, Neither hath this man sinned, nor his parents: but that the works of God should be made manifest in him" (Jn 9:2-3). Jesus said that his illness was *not* the result of sin.

However, we also find in Mark's gospel (2:1-12) that, when Jesus encountered the man sick of the palsy, He forgave his sin first and then healed him. Jesus dealt with his wickedness and then relieved his weakness. Sometimes illness may be a result of sin; however, sickness and sin are obviously not always related.

Neither do these verses in James 5 condemn the use of means or medicine for healing. Some people believe and teach that Christians should have nothing to do whatsoever with the medical profession—no doctors, no medicine, no hospitals, no human means at all. The Bible does *not* teach this. In fact, many scholars would suggest that the anointing oil of verse 14 was actually used as a medicine. We are told in Luke 10:34 that the good Samaritan applied oil to the wounds of the dying man he found on the road to Jericho. Much of the historical literature of that day confirms the fact that oil *was* used as a healing remedy.

But whether or not James is referring here to the use of

medicine, we do find that there are many references to medicine made throughout the Word of God. In Proverbs 17:22 we read, "A merry heart doeth good like a medicine." And if medicine and doctors are to be avoided, as some would teach, why was Paul associated with Luke, a member of the medical profession? In Colossians 4:14 Paul refers to his co-worker as, "Luke, the beloved physician." We even find that Paul prescribed a little medicine himself. Writing to Timothy who was suffering from stomach trouble, the apostle suggested that he, "Drink no longer water, but use a little wine for thy stomach's sake and thine often infirmities" (1 Ti 5:23).

Actually Jesus settled the matter plainly. In Matthew 9:12 our Lord declared, "They that be whole need not a physician, but they that are sick." Jesus clearly stated that sick people need a doctor.

So we see that James is not suggesting that sickness is always the result of sin. Nor do we find here—or in any other part of the Bible—that we are to avoid the medical profession. The child of God acts in wisdom as he utilizes the means of healing which are provided for him.

Second, notice what *is* taught in this passage. On the positive side, let me ask three questions concerning divine healing: (1) Is God able to heal? (2) Does God ever heal? and (3) Does God always heal?

Is God able to heal?

Certainly there is no hesitation in our answer to this question. There can be but one answer. The all-powerful God who created us can just as easily heal our bodies if it is His will. Without question we believe God *is able* to heal.

Does God ever heal?

Here too, there would be but few who would question

God's active participation in the area of divine healing. The Word of God clearly records the exercise of God's power in the healing of the sick. Not only was this true when our Lord was upon earth, but also during the centuries which have elapsed since He left.

I have experienced God's miraculous healing power even in my own life. During my student days at the Moody Bible Institute, I was seriously stricken with a malignant tumor. I was subjected to thirty radium treatments. For many weeks I was confined to a hospital bed, and the doctors told me that I possibly would not live.

Right there in my hospital room I prayed, "O God, this bed is my altar. My life is in Your hands. I subject myself to Your will." That was nearly thirty years ago. God performed a *miracle* in my life that confounded even the doctors. Yes, God is able to heal, and He *does heal* in many miraculous ways.

Is it always the will of god to heal?

To this question I would answer a definite no! There are some dear folk, however, who would answer with an emphatic yes. They contend that it is God's will to heal all sickness, that only sin or lack of faith keeps us from being healed. They would say that when Jesus Christ atoned for our sins on the cross He brought deliverance for all our infirmities.

Christ's death did bring about spiritual deliverance. It did cover the infirmities of sin. But nowhere do we find the promise of complete physical deliverance until Jesus Christ comes again to earth in power and glory. It is in that day that we are told, "God shall wipe away all tears from their eyes; and there shall be no more death, neither sorrow, nor crying, neither shall there be any more pain: for the former things are passed away" (Rev 21:4).

But to suggest that, if we now have sufficient faith, we can be healed of all sickness and disease is a dangerous position to take. For that matter, to argue that the healing of our infirmities depends solely on our faith would also suggest that, if our faith were great enough, we would never have to die.

As we study the gospels, we find that Jesus' miracles of healing were always done for a particular *spiritual* purpose. On several occasions our Lord selected a particular person to be healed out of a host of those who were afflicted. In John 5 we are told that a great multitude of sick people had gathered beside the pool of Bethesda seeking a cure for their illnesses. But Jesus chose just one man to be healed—and on a particular day, the Sabbath. Our Lord could have easily cured the entire lot of afflicted people, but He chose just one man that He might expose the false teachings of the religious leaders of that day, and that He might show Himself as Lord of the Sabbath. Christ's acts of healing were a demonstration of His deity.

What we find in God's Word is that our heavenly Father *is* concerned for His children. He *may* grant healing, if, in His wisdom, that is best. But in many cases He allows His children to suffer. This does not indicate lack of faith on their part, nor a lack of love on God's part. Sometimes we can learn more of God's way in sickness than in health, and often we can glorify Him more in suffering than we can in health and prosperity.

The apostle Paul was one whom God used greatly through his affliction. Paul was apparently half blind. He had to dictate his letters because he was unable to write except in a huge scrawl. To the church at Corinth he wrote that "lest I should be exalted above measure through the abundance of the revelations, there was given to me a thorn in the flesh, the messenger of Satan to buffet me, lest I should be exalted above measure. For this thing I besought the Lord thrice, that it might depart from me. And he said unto me, My grace is sufficient for thee" (2 Co 12:7-9).

In Romans 8:22-27 Paul speaks of our physical infirmities and tells us that we know not *how to pray.* "Likewise the Spirit also helpeth our infirmities: for we know not what we should pray for as we ought: but the Spirit itself maketh intercession for us with groanings which cannot be uttered. And he that searcheth the hearts knoweth what is the mind of the Spirit, because he maketh intercession for the saints according to the will of God" (Ro 8:26-27). Since the Holy Spirit makes intercession for the infirmed saints according to God's will, who are we to pray any other way?

We clearly see, then, that it is not *always* God's will to heal. It is God's will, however, that we pray for healing. "Is any sick among you?" says James, "let him call for the elders of the church; and let them pray over him . . . and the prayer of faith shall save the sick" (Ja 5:14-15). I do not believe that this refers to *ordinary prayer* no matter how good and earnest it may be. On one occasion even Paul said that he had to leave behind his fellow laborer, Trophimus, because he was sick (2 Ti 4:20). I am sure that Paul must have earnestly prayed for his afflicted friend. But, in my thinking, the "prayer of faith" cannot be prayed simply at will. It is given of God in certain cases to serve His purposes and to accomplish His sovereign will.

Hebrews 11 lists the great heroes of the Christian faith. Some, says the writer, "stopped the mouths of lions," some "quenched the violence of fire," some "escaped the edge of the sword," and received mighty deliverance from the hand of the Lord (Heb 11:33-34). But, we are also told, some were "tortured," some received "scourging," some were "sawn asunder," some were "tempted . . . afflicted . . . destitute." And yet these "all . . . obtained a good report through faith" (Heb 11:35-39).

Why were some of these heroes of faith delivered while others were tormented? Because some had faith and others had none? No! They all had faith. They all believed in the same God, but God's will was not accomplished in the same way through them all.

Can God heal us in our afflictions? Yes, He is able, and He at times works miraculously in the lives of some of His servants. But is there healing for us all? No, my friend, not until one day we receive that glorious resurrected body Christ has promised to them that know and love Him.

Until that day, may we with the hymn writer, Benjamin Schmolck, say:

> My Jesus, as Thou wilt: O may Thy will be mine!
> Into Thy hand of love I would my all resign.
> Through sorrow or thro' joy, Conduct me as Thine own,
> And help me still to say, "My Lord, Thy will be done."
>
> My Jesus, as Thou wilt: All shall be well for me;
> Each changing future scene I gladly trust with Thee.
> Straight to my home above I travel calmly on,
> And sing in life or death, "My Lord, Thy will be done."

- "Is any among you afflicted? let him pray. Is any merry? let him sing psalms" (Ja 5:13).

- What are we to do with our great emotional conflicts in life? James tells us to relate them to God!

- Sometimes illness may be a result of sin; however, sickness and sin are obviously not always related (Jn 9:2-3).

- If medicine and doctors are to be avoided, as some would teach, why was Paul associated with Luke, a member of the medical profession?

- Is it always the will of God to heal? To this question I would answer a definite no!

- Since the Holy Spirit makes intercession for the infirmed saints according to God's will, who are we to pray any other way? (Ro 8:22-27).

- In my thinking, the "prayer of faith" cannot be prayed simply at will. It is given of God in certain cases to serve His purpose and to accomplish His sovereign will.

- Why were some of these heroes of faith delivered while others were tormented—because some had faith and others had none? No! They all had faith. They all believed in the same God, but God's will was not accomplished in the same way through them all.